3 1336 00419 2994

D0944358

"I Believe, But . . . !"

230

"I Believe, But . . . !"

A REAFFIRMATION OF FAITH

by

WALTER R. COURTENAY

SAN DIEGO PUBLIC LIBRARY

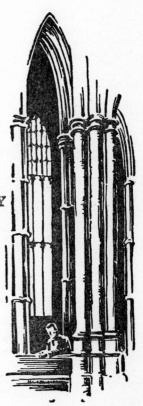

John Knox Press

RICHMOND
VIRGINIA

Copyright, 1950, by John Knox Press
Printed in the United States of America
158-(1)-11135

Contents

MAR 1 5 1963

ह৵

Foreword

A BETTER WORLD and a stronger, purer, more virile Christian Church cannot be erected on the marshy ground of modern doubt or born from the womb of intellectualized indifference. There is only one enduring foundation for faith, and that foundation is none other than the life and love of Jesus Christ as we know Him in the New Testament. By neglecting Him, the words of His lips and the spirit of His living, we have endangered the whole of mankind.

Some two years ago a friend said to me, "The trouble with modern Christians is this: they want to condition everything they believe. Hence, every church member recites the Apostles' Creed in these words, 'I believe in God, but . . .,' 'I believe in Jesus Christ, but . . .' Now how can you get a dynamic Christianity out of this vast program of evasion?"

This series of sermons is a condemnation of this program of evasion, and while it is not in any way a serious attempt to interpret the great Creed, it does seek to share the thoughts that have enriched my life and made it to overflow with a consciousness of His greatness.

The years have convinced me of one thing: the Christian life can best be expressed by two words, "credo" and "amo." God, Himself, hath made these one in Christ and man can separate them only at the expense of his own peace.

Many today cry "credo," and their voices are strident and harsh. Their ultraorthodox minds make taut and belligerent the lips through which they speak. One listens in vain to hear the overtones of a compassionate heart, and looks in vain to find the eyes of tenderness.

Others cry "amo," but their voices are as strident and harsh as those who raise the battle cry of "credo." These are the ultraliberals. They are as belligerent and determined in their cry of "I love" as the others are who cry "I believe." In neither do we find often the tenderness and constructive understanding of Jesus.

As I know Him, He expressed "credo" through the medium of "amo." "Credo" was the skeleton structure that gave size and shape to His message, but "amo" was the flesh that rounded it out and gave it grace and loveliness. Together "credo" and "amo" formed the most attractive life of history.

The Church is again becoming theology-conscious, and it is well, but the Church must never forget that theology and sociology are twins, made so by God Himself. What we believe must be matched by a way of life that gives reality to what we believe. The Christ who taught also loved, and the world remembers what He said almost entirely because it cannot forget how He lived.

Jesus Christ was more than a man. The religion that we have received from Him is more than a man-made scheme of salvation. It is of God. The great words He spoke, and the tremendous influence He has exerted on civilization, form a mystery that we are permitted to see, but not to understand.

Let not the "datedness" of Christianity move us to label it senile. Christianity has its own theory of relativity, and by it we are convinced that as the lines of truth are followed today and tomorrow they move in a circle and finally bring us home to God. All truth has a common source and a single objective. He said, "I am the truth."

WALTER ROWE COURTENAY

First Presbyterian Church
Nashville, Tennessee

"I Believe, But . . . !"

"I Believe in Faith, But . . ."

(HEBREWS 11:1-6)

ᘐᕉ

MODERN MAN is allergic to the word "faith." To him it is an irritant. The sound of it, the sight of it, makes him break out in a scarlet rash.

Twentieth-century man feels he is self-sufficient. He contends that he is not uninformed as were his ancestors. He has read, heard lectures, participated in discussions, and observed the history of man. He is no longer a credulous creature of crippled intellect. He is the creator of the most fabulous era of history, the age of science, the age of atomic power. He is a pragmatist. What works is good, and right is a matter of utility. He boasts that he lives by facts and logic, and not by faith which has neither facts nor logic.

This modern man seeks to cast off the anchor lines of religion and morality. He wants freedom from God to be added to the other freedoms of life; nay, he would make freedom from God to be the first of the basic freedoms of the earth. Hence this indifference to, or open scorn of, religious faith. He calls it infantile credulity, belief based on fallacy, faith founded on untruth, superstition in an age of science. He feels no sting from retaliatory conscience. He feels no need of saving grace. Believing that man is an animal he regrets but accepts the brute in man. Evolution, he says, will eventually solve the moral problems of the race, for man is surely ascending toward nobler humanity. Since God had nothing to do with the creation of matter and of life, since He did not create man in His own image, modern man feels free to ignore God, to call Him uncomplimentary names, and to discount generously the place of religion and faith in normal life. He laughingly states that the Church reminds him of Columbus, who went forth not knowing where he was going; when he got there he did not know where he was; when he got back home he did not know where he had been; and all on someone else's money.

Of course the story is clever, but it is not as funny as modern man believes, for Columbus was above all else a man of great faith. Taking the knowledge he had, he surmised the existence of other lands, and although he had never seen them, walked on them, or named them, he believed they were there, far off across the uncharted sea, and hence the sailing of his ships into the unknown. His faith was based on knowledge, but his knowledge was but a port of departure. His faith meant very little, and the knowledge was of small value, until he cleared the harbor and pointed his ships toward the open sea. It was the going forth into the unknown that gave evidence of the faith that trusts and conquers.

FAITH IS A PART OF ALL TRUE PROGRESS

These observations lead me to point out that without faith there is no progress, no brilliant discoveries, no glorious achievements, no high attainment.

Mr. Kenneth Goode, a New York businessman, has helped many, many persons rise to places of success in that great city. To each inquirer he says, "How can I get you a job? Just sit back and forget you are looking for a job. Skip all that. Think ten or twelve years from now. What would you like to be at that time of life? If everything worked out favorably, what would you like to be?"

In other words, men should think in terms of goals and not jobs. Jobs should be milestones on our way to goals, but the goals are the important objectives of living.

Evolution concerns itself with goals. If the theory be true, what is the final goal toward which we move? What is God trying to achieve? Is God going to be satisfied with mere man, man just above the beasts of the field and forest, or is God going to be dissatisfied until man is just a littler lower than the angels?

I say to you that it is spiritual man that marks the goal of evolution, man at one with God, man the companion of God, man in complete harmony with God. Man, and we have every honest right to believe it, came into existence by the will of God, regardless of what method you favor, and God has a goal for man, and the goal of man is godlikeness, not brutelikeness. That is why God sent His Son into the world to seek and to save mankind, for it is only by such a method that we can know how man ought to live and what men ought to be. God in Jesus Christ has made clear our goal, and every thinking person, every true evolutionist, should accept the fact without hesitancy.

Christianity comes to give science two answers: Man began with God as did all life. Man must end with God as must all life. At the beginning man and Maker lived in closest harmony. At the end man and Maker should live in sweetest fellowship. Science and education should be striving to create Christlike people in a Kingdom world, and as long as science and education ignore the Christ goal of evolution, their knowledge of beginnings and developments are of little importance.

Nearer to the thesis is the fact that science itself cannot operate without faith, for every experiment is a venturing forth from truth known to truth that may be known. Faraday was right when, in the laboratory, he said to his friends, "Gentlemen, remove your hats, I am about to ask God a question." Dr. Ligon of Union College says that such questioning is in reality prayer, for when the inner life of the scientist is brought into close relationship with God in an experiment, he is praying as surely as when a Christian kneels to petition guidance.

All seeking for truth, be it scientific or religious, theistic or secular, is an act of faith. The surmise that there is greater truth to be known is the only path whereby we move from the known to the surmised. This is rudimentary faith, to be sure, but it is faith. It may indicate that the deep urge of a man's spirit is wiser than his head. A man may easily hold the hem of God's celestial garment in his hands and never know it. Many may offer up the unworded urges of the soul as prayer without being conscious of their search for Him who desires that the secrets of the universe and the soul be found and shared. Science, like all other seekers for truth, must follow the God-path of the brain and heart regardless of the names he uses. He must always move from evidence of truth to truth itself. That is an act of faith.

Faith, in its true Christian usage, may be defined as belief based on evidence, belief based on knowledge. Faith is not believing what is unprovable, what is not so! Like science, we know in part, and we prophesy in part. We begin with what we know, ask questions regarding what may be known, and then venture forth toward the undiscovered continents.

The writer of the letter to the Hebrews was both Christian and scientific when he said that "the seen is born of the unseen, and the visible of the invisible."[1] That is true of chemistry, physics, *and* Christianity. It was good science and religion 1900 years ago, and it is good science and religion today. Without faith there is no progress, for only by faith do we move from what is to what may be.

FAITH IS PART OF ALL BASIC HUMAN RELATIONSHIPS

Columbus sailed for the New World because certain people had faith in Columbus. Certain people sailed with him because they had faith in Columbus. His theories about navigation and geography were not understood by those who trusted him, yet they trusted him. They had faith in him.

All basic human relationships are based on faith. What would we do without our friends who are as firesides on dull days, lights in the darkness, shade in the heat of summer, shelter in storm, and comfort in our sorrows? A man is only as strong as his friends. And what is friendship? Is it not faith in others who have faith in us?

When young people stand before me to be made one in marriage, what does it mean? They say they love each other and desire to be made one before God and man, but is not love itself affection based on faith between persons? Can there be love when there is no faith? The man does not really know the girl he is about to marry, nor does she really know him. Neither knows what the future holds of wonder or surprise, but each, knowing a little about the other, is willing to trust the unknown and to set sail for the distant islands. That is faith.

All business is conducted on the basis of faith. Banks, investment houses, commercial concerns, industry, all the business of our nation, is conducted on faith. Without faith there could be no contracts, no agreements, no commitments, no courts.

Even the funeral service is an act of faith. When we stand at the open graves of our loved ones and place their bodies in the embrace of Mother Earth, we do so with faith in God who has promised us life that shall deathless be. We lay them to rest with sorrow, yet with hope, and our hope is based on the life and words of Him who conquered sin and death, even Jesus.

All that is good between people, all that we say, all that we do, is evidence of our faith in one another — even the agreements made between murderers and thieves — for without faith we can do nothing, and without faith all is chaos.

The international problems of today find their source in the lack of faith between nations. The industrial disturbances of the world are based on lack of faith between capital and labor. The rivalries of ideologies are evidence of lack of faith between parties.

When men lose faith, homes are broken, partnerships dissolved, businesses ruined, classes in conflict, and nations at war. All the basic relationships of life are based on faith, even our religious faith, for our religious faith is based on God's faith in us.

FAITH IS PART OF OUR RICHER MATURITY

Like all forms of life man moves from simplicity to complexity, and complexity in man should stand for higher values, nobler possibilities and attainments. Life should not be mere sailing across uncharted seas. It should also mean arrivals and discoveries. For all of us there should be days when we find branches and fresh berries on the water, and behold in the darkness lights on new shore lines. Life should not be sailing in the midst of a rebellious crew forever fearing tomorrow. We should so live and sail that even the rebellious ones will be brought to the New World and made to kneel beneath the flying banners of discovery. He who has no inner urge to cross the seas and find new worlds will never know the glow of faith. He who makes no great discoveries must live in the stale air of sensuous rooms with only artificial lights aglow. Secular living, sensuous living, sensate living, is never great living.

When I was a child I had what I would call *natural* faith. I accepted my parents as my parents without proof. I ate my food without fear of its being poisoned or contaminated. I knew that when I was thirsty there would be water, milk, or lemonade. I knew that a bed awaited my tired body, clothes my cold body, friendliness my moments of aloneness, fear, and hurt. Everything about me was taken for granted and I found no need of asking questions about the normal routine of living. The beauty of the earth thrilled me. The mystery of seasons and stars filled me with a pleasant awe. The love of loved ones wrapped me warmly in an embrace of sweet contentment. I had faith as a child, but it was the faith of the animal kingdom — natural faith.

The years have proved that natural faith is not enough, and in the course of development my natural faith has become *informed* faith, belief based on knowledge. I have no fear of the earth's crust giving way beneath my feet and plunging me into the fiery abyss. I feel sure that the earth will continue to turn on its axis once in every twenty-four hours, giving me day and darkness. I have no question but that the world will continue to be tilted at its present angle, thus maintaining the present temperatures. I do not worry about the moon coming closer to the earth and pulling my world apart or that the wonderful arrangement of oxygen and carbon dioxide, oxygen and hydrogen, will change. Knowledge has made me secure in the universe, and in the universe I find every evidence of the presence of my Father, God.

Who else placed my earth near enough to the sun to be warmed and healed, yet far enough away to prevent our being reduced to ashes? Who prevents our drifting farther away and thus being reduced to ice? Who placed the moon where it would give us reflected glory, and raise and lower the seas, without destruction to our earth? Who arranged events so that animals breathe in oxygen and breathe out carbon dioxide while plants breathe in carbon dioxide and breathe out oxygen? Who foresaw the fact that of all the heavenly bodies our earth would be the only one to produce and maintain life? Who surrounded this tiny world with its protecting belt of air so that the millions of pieces of flying star stuff do not destroy us? Who was wise enough to see to it that oxygen was here in the amount of 21 per cent and nitrogen 78 per cent so that life as we know it could exist?[2]

I tell you that this is in truth my Father's world! I find Him everywhere in the laws of chemistry and physics, zoology and biology, genes and giant stars. "It is he that hath made us, and not we ourselves."[3]

Even as God has been active in the field of nature, thus raising my faith from natural faith to informed faith, so He has been active in human nature to bring to us a revelation of Himself. We find Him in the shining of His stars, we mark Him in the flowering of the fields, but we know Him best in Jesus Christ, His Son!

Natural faith is of the animal world. Informed faith is of the world of natural man. We need another faith, *a transforming faith*, a faith that actually helps us achieve the goal of creation, the goal of evolution, the goal of God: twice-born men, men of Christ, children of the living God. Natural faith gave me intimations of such a relationship, for the seasons taught me and the fields whispered and the stars sang together. Instinctively I looked up in an attitude of faith. I felt but I did not know. Informed faith gave me many evidences of the Creator and His matchless artistry. Science has been the archeologist digging away the debris and disclosing the walls and streets of God's world. The principles of nature and of human nature spoke learnedly and convincingly. Instinctively I bowed my head before knowledge so radiant and glittering. Once more I felt I knew a little more, but I was not sure.

Then came transforming faith. Then came Jesus! I had heard of Him with the hearing of the ear, but suddenly I saw Him walking midst the rosy mists of dawn. O what a beautiful morning! It was truly dawn in my soul! His purity made me conscious of my impurity. His wisdom made me conscious of my ignorance. I saw His goodness o'ertower mine as blue skies rise above scarred earth. His gentleness and tenderness made me weep, and His understanding of people softened me. When I saw Him betrayed I wanted to slay the ingrate Judas, and when He hung upon the cross I knelt and sobbed. Like the penitent thief I could only say, "We receive the due reward of our deeds: but this man hath done nothing amiss."[4]

> "Love so amazing, so divine,
> Demands my soul, my life, my all."[5]

As the writer said of Abel, "By his faith he is speaking to us still";[6] just so does Jesus speak. Even as Enoch died young, being taken of God in the full fresh strength of manhood, so

Jesus died. Even as Abraham went out not knowing whither he went, but trusting Him who called and guided him, so went Jesus, and both lived in tents, believing that life here on earth is but a pilgrimage to a home beyond the vale of death.

Transforming faith teaches me that I am immortal, and that it is within my power to possess deathless life and eternal love. It tells me that though my sins be as scarlet, they can be as white as snow.[7] It tells me that I can be harmonized with God, united with God, related to God as a child is related to its father, so that I have victory over sin and death; that if I have faith, I can remove mountains!

Impossible? Dr. Alexis Carrel did not think so. Dr. A Cressy Morrison does not think so. Dr. Lecomte du Noüy and Compton do not think so. Science is advancing today in full support of God, His place in the universe, and evolution's goal — spiritual man!

Jesus lived the life. He taught men that the life was open to them, and that He would give them power to live the life. He promised forgiveness and life everlasting to all who believed.

I know Him. I know many who have trusted Him. I know what faith has done for them. Why should I not believe? If the goal of living is godlikeness why should I hesitate?

I do not hesitate. I bow and call Him, Lord. I strive each day to know a little more of His wisdom and His love. I fellowship with Him in prayer. I witness for Him, striving to teach the world the Golden Goal and the Golden Path to the Golden Goal. I give, and I get. I share, and possess the more. I empty myself, but am never emptied. I live, yet not I, for Christ liveth in me. The personal pronoun is in evidence because I speak, not for myself alone, but for all who have accepted Him, for all who have sailed and found and returned.

Is it all a myth, a poetic dream lacking reality, a child's story filled with impossible wonders? Some years ago a Greenland Eskimo was taken to New York as a reward for faithful service in one of our Arctic exploration parties. When he returned home he told his people about the buildings that rise like mountains, of the canyons called streets, of trains that are lived in like houses, but move like rushing reindeer. He told them about movies and electric lights, subways and airplanes. The people listened, grew sullen, and walked away. They gave the man a new name, a name that was his name thereafter, The Liar.

Did their lack of belief mean that there was no New York and all the wonders the Eskimo described? Did the people of Spain believe all that Columbus and his companions related when they returned from the great journey? Should we be surprised that the unbelieving world finds it difficult to believe Jesus and the apostles, you and me?

A. J. Cronin, author of *The Citadel, The Keys of the Kingdom,* and *The Green Years,* is actually a medical man. The time came when he had to go to a small village in Scotland and lead a quiet life in order to recover his health. He hated the place, its quietness and its sullen peaks. It was while there that he suddenly decided to write a novel. He had always thought he could, and now he decided to make the attempt. For months he worked on the story and finished it, but the end brought no sense of gladness and accomplishment. When he read it over it seemed puerile and amateurish, so much so that he threw it into the wastepaper basket in disgust and went forth a discouraged man. When he reached the edge of the farm he came upon old Angus, the owner of the little farm, and a man who loved all that had to do with the mind of man. Dr. Cronin told Angus of his failure, declaring with emphasis that he would never try to write another line. Old Angus stopped digging in the drainage ditch and looked at him and said, "No doubt you're the one that's right, doctor, and I'm the one that's wrong. My father ditched this bog all his days and never made a pasture. I've dug it all my days and I've never made a pasture. But pasture or no pasture, I canna help but dig. For my father knew and I know that if you only dig enough a pasture can be made here."[8]

I dare not stand before my chaotic, discouraged, secularized, pagan world and say to other men, "I believe in faith, but . . ." I must say to them as old Angus said to Cronin, "My Father knows and I know that if we only dig enough a pasture can be made of this bog of earth."

Yes, I know it looks silly at this time, this work of trying to drain the world of sin, but I cannot help but pray, "Thy kingdom come. Thy will be done in earth," and I cannot help but speak the Word and give the prayer and live the life that may one day drain the bog and build green pastures in the earth!

O Christ of living faith, O Christ who taught men faith, O Christ of wisdom and of love, help Thou our unbelief. O give us faith!

CHAPTER TWO

"I Believe in Prayer, But..."

(MATTHEW 6:5-15)

ह॰

ALMOST ALL modern Christians begin a discussion on prayer with the words, "I believe in prayer, but . . ." One can almost see the mental gears getting ready to slip into neutral or reverse, for few "modern" Christians care to sound assured when they speak of prayer.

It is the observation of many that on the whole the church has ceased to be a "house of prayer." From all points of the compass one hears reports concerning the prayerlessness of modern Christianity. Prayer has become the lost art of the church.

In recent years our churches have made some remarkable advances. Our buildings are more attractive, more usable, more strategically located. Church programs are determined after proper advice from trained educators and psychologists. Teaching materials are graded and prepared by skilled leaders. Activities from the Nursery Department to the adult levels are guided by well-defined objectives. We have advanced in all departments of church life save one, the department of prayer. There we are in a period of dark recession. We teach people everything except the one thing they need above all else, how to pray.

Jesus believed in prayer. He prayed. He taught men to pray. He said that men ought always to pray and not to faint, and that all life can be conditioned to high nobility and usefulness by prayer.

Those who walked with Him learned the lessons well, so well that they went forth and conquered a pagan world, and by prayer, and prayerful living, defeated the Roman Empire.

I am in the ministry today because I was literally prayed into it. Through the prayers of loved ones and friends I was called, cleansed, and commissioned a messenger of the Gospel. I did not choose the ministry. Left to myself, it was the last vocation I would have chosen, but I had no choice. People prayed me into it. More than that: whatever success has been mine in my efforts to instruct and inspire, challenge and comfort, guide and guard, has resulted from the prayers of others. I thank God for the little children, the young people, the parents, and especially the shut-ins who daily take my name upon their lips in prayer. Without them I could do nothing. They are an inherent part of my Christian ministry. Blessed is the man who is remembered in prayer by his friends.

WHAT IS PRAYER?

But what is prayer? Is it a good practice or a bad problem? A childish whim or a wise man's way?

Mark Twain once observed that everyone talks about the weather but no one does anything about it. He might have added that most Christians talk about prayer, but very few pray. There is abroad in the lives of people many quack theories of prayer and many quack practices. To most people prayer is a grocery list that one telephones to Heaven's Supermarket, the reading of the list being climaxed with the words, "I need these things right away, in fact, right now!" God is the errand boy whose sole job is the delivering of orders from the earth.

When some folks pray, they deal in history and geography. They are bent on teaching God something about the size and shape of the earth and acquainting Him with the history of the human family. Even though they recognize in soberer moments that the earth is as familiar to God as Gabriel's wings, they still persist in making clear to Him the particular events in their smaller sphere of interest that seem to be escaping His attention.

Prayer for many is the long-distance telephone call that is reserved for death messages. Prayer is the telegram that is never used save in instances of serious illness. Prayer is the fire extinguisher we hang on the wall for that rare hour of danger when its services will be needed. Prayer is the spare tire in the trunks of our cars, of no interest to us save in the hour when a puncture or blowout has "let us down." Prayer for most Christians is a call for help in life's emergencies.

A test was given recently to forty-five university and seminary students.[1] They were all regular church attenders, and most of them were Presbyterian or Episcopalian. They were asked to react to six situations. Would you pray, asked the questions, if —

1. Your child were sick, probably dying?
2. Your employer's business failed, leaving you facing the later years of life without security?
3. You were on a ship in a storm and you were in danger of being washed overboard?
4. You were walking through the country on a beautiful spring morning and felt unusually good?
5. You had waited two weeks for a letter that was most important to your future and the letter suddenly came bringing a favorable reply?
6. You had to do a piece of creative writing, and after much worry and work, you produced a favorable article?

The report showed that even these enlightened persons, many of them future ministers, prayed only from necessity.

When they could not control the circumstances of life, they prayed. Prayer to them was a matter of "the eleventh hour."

Prayer is an emergency measure in the lives of most of us, but it ought not to be. As Christians we should approach prayer from a richer background of thought and understanding. I come to prayer with these thoughts in mind. I believe that God is the Creator of the universe and all that is therein. I believe that He is a Person, a Person who has manifested Himself to man in nature, in human nature, in history, and in Jesus Christ. I believe that millions of years have gone into God's creative plan and that Christian man is the highest attainment of creation, and that God is especially interested in those who are brothers to the Christ.

If these things be true, then it must follow that God has also prepared a way whereby we may talk with Him. He made us to be talking animals, but is not He a hearing God? We have power to ask. Does not He have power to answer? Is not the mouth of man and the ear of God a unit, made so by divine authority, whereby there may be intercourse between the human and the divine?

Prayer thus becomes *companionship with God*. Prayer is the path whereby we ascend into the presence of Him who is our delight. Prayer ought to tell us that we should love God just because He is God; we should be with Him often, consciously and constantly remembering His wonderful love and vitalizing wisdom. We should not come always asking, and most times, only asking, but we should come just to be near Him and to feel the enrichment of His holy affection.

Prayer should also mean *conversation*. Prayer ought to mean visiting with a friend, just talking about things.

F. W. Boreham tells the story of the minister who made a hospital call on a sick Scotsman. When he entered and was seated, he noticed another chair on the other side of the bed, a chair placed as if some friend had just used it and departed. "Well, Donald," said the minister, pointing to the empty chair, "I see you have recently had a visitor." The Scotsman looked surprised and then smiled. "Aye," he said, "you mean the chair. I'll tell you about that. Years ago I found that I could not pray. It had lost its power. When I knelt I was so tired that I invariably fell asleep. It troubled me greatly, and so I told my minister about it and he said not to kneel any more, but to sit on a chair and place another chair in front of me; to imagine that Jesus was sitting there, and then to talk with Him as I would to a friend. That I did, and across the years that have followed that has been my method of prayer, and that is why the chair is here in my room."

Two weeks later he died and his daughter called on the minister and said, "Father is dead. When I went to his room, he was lying there fast asleep in death. He hadn't moved since I left him, except that for some reason unknown to me, he had put his hand on the chair by the bed. Do you understand?" "Yes," said the minister, "I understand."

So do we, don't we? We know that when we pray we must sit face to face with Jesus and talk to Him as one talks with a trusted and greatly loved friend.

Prayer is also *cleansing*. These lives of ours get so dirty. The soul of man becomes a disordered room with dingy windows and dusty walls and dirty floors, and when man comes to God in prayer, the windows are cleaned, the walls are wiped down and the floors swept, and man rises from his knees ordered for better living.

Oh, prayer is so many, many things. Prayer is just leaning back on God when one is tired of life's struggle. Prayer is putting up the shades and letting the light from above stream into one's life. Prayer is flipping the light switch when the day is done and the darkness comes. Prayer is stepping under the warm shower and feeling one's body being caressed into cleanliness. Prayer is a cup of cold water on a hot day that is sweet in the mouth and healing to the whole body. Prayer is a brief vacation when one is weary from life's routine. Prayer is a friendly voice in an hour of loneliness. Prayer is a reaffirmation of faith in a doubting world. Prayer is a state of mind concerning God and the future of man.

Jesus once said, "Seek ye first the kingdom of God, and his righteousness; and all these things shall be added unto you."[2] I have come to feel that this is a wonderful symbol of prayer, for when we seek Him just because He is our heavenly Father, just because He is our God and our best companion, the things are given us without our asking. Jesus also said, "What shall it profit a man, if he shall gain the whole world, and lose his own soul?"[3] Aye, if we seek only the things of the Father we will not get the Father, but if we seek the Father surely we will get the things we need, for what is a lost soul but a soul filled with things, and empty of God.

Prayer is companionship with God. Prayer is conversation with God. Prayer is cleansing. Prayer is success in noble living.

WHAT CAN PRAYER MEAN TO A MODERN MAN?

You may be saying to yourself, "That is all very well, my friend. It is beautiful poetry, but is it fact? Can a modern man believe it? After all, this is the age of science. We live by law. Black magic is no more and white magic never was! You cannot expect a modern man to believe that prayer can make God change His mind just for the sake of an individual."

But who knows God? Who knows what God will and will not do? Who knows all the laws of life and the universe?

Dare science become boastful and arrogant just because it has found a few of God's laws, laws which God Himself placed in the earth? Dare a man holding a branch in his hand boast that he is now lord of the forests? Men discover laws, but men do not make them! Who knows all the laws of this strange world?

Others may say, "But this is the age of psychology. Men have examined the human mind. They know it well, and they can explain these tricks of worship and of prayer. Is not prayer after all our reaction to fear? Is not prayer a way of escaping life's problems and the day's responsibilities?"

Doubtless it is in some instances, but it was not so with Jesus. He lived with God as companion and friend, and when He knelt in Gethsemane it was not new ground for Him. He had prayed in that very spot many, many times. There He and God had talked together as friends, and when one is in trouble, should he not return to the place of friendship and share his woe with one who understands? Mark this and mark it well: It is true that Jesus sought to avoid the cup, but when it was not withdrawn, He took it and drank it empty. In the long, slow hours of the night when He moved from the Garden to the home of Caiaphas, to the palace of Herod, to the halls of Pilate, He did not pray for escape. On that first Good Friday, when injustice was rampant, He did not avoid the eyes of Pilate, the threats of the mob, the scourge of the soldiers, or the insults of the priests. When He walked the Via Doloroso He carried the cross without bitterness or pity, and when they drove the nails into His hands and raised His body on that tree of torture, there was no outcry. After hanging there three hours, He still did not ask for release or sudden death, but prayed for God's mercy on His foes, and led a thief into Paradise.

Escape? Many of you served in the American forces during the recent war. You flew the planes, manned the ships, rode the tanks, and marched in the ranks. Did you pray for escape? Or did you pray for courage and faith to do what must be done? Did you not kneel and pray for a brave man's heart and a Christian's faith, and did you not soar into the heights, launch out into the deep, ride roaringly forward, and attack the foe, ever going nearer to danger and death?

Escape? Christian prayer at its best is never for escape, but for courage and for faith to confront the problems and the pain with stalwart trust. Let not the psychiatrist believe that he has become God. He does not know all. Dr. George Buttrick tells us that one of the leading doctors of America kept a chart on the patients he sent to a psychiatrist. Twenty came back improved. Twenty came back worse. Sixty came back without change.

When I want to know something about chemistry, I talk to a chemist who knows chemistry. When I want to know something about engineering, I talk to a skilled engineer. When I want to know something about music, I had better talk with those who know that field and live therein.

Why then should we go to prayerless scientists and psychologists for information concerning prayer? The only person who knows whether prayer works or not is the person who prays, the person who has made himself an authority in the field of prayer. Jesus was such an authority, so much so, that the disciples came to Him saying, "Lord, teach us to pray." Those men had prayed from childhood. As good Jews, they prayed every day, but in Jesus they found a new concept of prayer. He lived so near to God that His very humanity became radiant with deity, and the disciples were conscious of the poverty of their own prayers and lives.

O Modern Man, you who tithe mint and anise and leave undone the weightier measures of the Law, why do you follow leaders who are prayerless and godless? How can you learn the better way of life from those who have lost it? Can an atheist instruct you in the truth of God, and can the agnostic give you knowledge concerning Christ? Must you continue to try to quench your thirst at the dry cisterns? Is not the confusion and disorder of our generation due to the fact that we have lost the path of prayer, which God created for us that we might live in companionship with Him who is the original scientist and the only true psychologist?

WHAT CAN PRAYER DO FOR MODERN SOCIETY?

Society needs people of character, and where shall we find them, nay, how shall we make them? Have we reached the place where we must choose science or religion, the psychologist or the priest? Nay, we must not! That is what many would have us do, knowing that our further confusion and destruction lie in that direction. There is no war between true science and true Christianity, nor is there conflict between true psychology and true prayer. The modern world needs truth from all sources and needs truth organized and harnessed for constructive living. Christianity needs science in order to build a better world, and science needs Christianity if we are to use the powers of science for the saving of mankind. Christianity needs psychologists if we are to mold better people, and psychologists need Christianity if the values of life are to be conserved for the improvement of the race. Working together we can build the golden age of man; working against each other we will drive humanity back to the jungle or wipe man from the face of the earth altogether.

In this scheme of things prayer is not a substitute for thinking or working, but prayer ought to help us have better thoughts and do better work. It ought to be the path to better selfhood and better society, for it must follow that all true prayer ends in social good. The man who habitually humbles himself before God, prays and works for nobler selfhood, harnesses himself in the program of God for a better race and a better world, must be of benefit to society, for such a man will not exploit his fellow man nor work according to the patterns of envy, covetousness, and greed. He who seeks to please God as Jesus did must be of value to all humanity.

There is in prayer a trinity of reconstruction that must not be ignored, for Christian prayer is pardon, Christian prayer is power, and Christian prayer is peace, and he whose life knows pardon, possesses power, and expresses itself in peace contains within himself the foundation of a new world order.

Man shall not live by bread alone, but by the Word of God. Man shall not live by might and power, but by the Spirit of the Christ, and hence by prayer. The great periods of Christian history have been periods of prayer, and only by prayer can the world be made new.

In that startling, revealing, challenging picture, "The Beginning or the End," one follows with increasing interest the story of the making of the first atomic bomb. The days of research are over. The scientists have done their work well and we stand on Tinian in the Marianas getting ready to drop the first bomb on Japan. Behind that moment are the best brains in the scientific world of Great Britain, Canada, and the United States. Behind that moment sprawl the giant plants like Oak Ridge. Behind that moment are the millions of tons of materials for plant and experiment. Behind that moment is a dream of harnessing the fundamental power of the universe. Now the B-29 is waiting to receive the bomb into its belly. The crews have been briefed, and all is in readiness. The scene changes and we live for a moment in another world. It is dawn and the crews of the bombers kneel on a hillside, each man holding in his hand a lighted candle. Faces are serious as the chaplain prays for the men with wings, the men who must carry that first bomb to Japan, for the men who must defy death. The chaplain says "Amen" and the men echo it, "Amen." In the following sequence we fly to Japan, drop the bomb on Hiroshima, watch the world writhe in death and die, and return.

As I left the theater the prayer service on the hillside at dawn stood out clear and strong. It seemed to be the burial service for the pre-atomic world and man's invocation to God for mercy upon the world of split atoms. In the picture there were two other prayers that stood out sharply. They were spoken that day in Chicago when chain reactions were definitely multiplied and men knew they could harness the power of the atom for purposes of war. Dr. Fermi prayed, "God give us time," and the young scientist from Columbia prayed, "God forgive us."

Is there a place in the modern world for prayer? Who shall win in the strange future that lies before us, those who pray for time in which to create new weapons wherewith to kill the world or those who pray for God's forgiveness for our sinful societies that will not learn the paths to brotherhood and peace? More than any former generation we must learn to say, "I believe in prayer," for if we do not believe and practice prayer, who shall protect us and save us from the wars of tomorrow?

O Father God, Companion of our hearts and Saviour of our souls, teach us to pray!

CHAPTER THREE

"I Believe in Love, But ... "

(1 JOHN 4:7-16)

ನ

CHRISTIANITY makes its appeal to the world on the basis of four fundamental claims:

1. It is the fullest expression of the love of God.
2. It has as its founder the most lovable and the most loving person that ever lived.
3. It possesses the richest literature on love and good-will known to man.
4. The world can be saved by love, and therefore by Christianity.

During my ministry I have defended these claims. I believe they are defendable. But I confess this day that few Christians and very few congregations actually strive to live on the basis of love. The human side of individual and corporate Christianity looms so large that one seldom sees the radiance of the divine. Entirely too much of modern Christianity is lived on the basis of, "Yes, I believe in love, but ... !"

I BELIEVE IN LOVE

In spite of the Church's almost studied indifference to love in action in daily activities; in spite of Dorothy Parker's threatening words, "Women and elephants never forget"; in spite of modern novels and movies which make love a fire in the body and not a flame in the soul, I believe in love.

I believe in love because I have seen it shining in the limpid eyes of a girl repeating after me the marriage vow. I have seen it in amethyst glory in the eyes of a young mother. I have read its poetic beauty in the face of many an elderly person who told me of that beloved partner who was already walking beyond the place called death.

I believe in love because I have seen it in the excited faces of little children, the eager faces of youth, and the confident faces of the old as they walked hand in hand into life's sunset.

I believe in love because I have seen it make harsh men gentle, bad men good, and good men better.

I believe in love because I have known doctors and teachers, ministers and farmers, businessmen and laborers, who have expressed in word and deed their active good will toward their fellow men.

I believe in love because Christianity gained its first victories through love. It was the love of Christian for Christian, and Christian for pagan, that first moved the ancient world to look twice in the direction of the Christ. It was Christianity's concern for the welfare of others that moved the Church into the very forefront of life. It was the Church's determination to transform a pagan world into the Kingdom of God that gave it divine momentum, and we are still coasting on the force of those early constructive years.

Who cared for the plague-stricken populations of the second century? The Christians! Who buried the pagan dead? The Christians! Who opened the first hospital in Europe? Gallincanus, a Christian! Who organized life for the lepers in the fourth century? The Christians! Who first took an interest in the unemployed? St. Basil, a Christian! Who gave his life to stop the brutality of the Roman arena? Telemachus, a Christian! Read the record of golden kindness and good will in the first six centuries of Christianity's drive to capture the world for God and you will find that the Gospel of Christ produced a social concern for mankind that made the Church a powerhouse of love.

I believe in love because I have seen the love of God in Christ. He who made the spinning spheres of heaven and molded the earth in His hands, He who created life and ordered its ascent, He who has wooed mankind with a sweetheart's tenderness, has made manifest to us His brightest attribute, His love.

Ah, yes, we stand and sing these words with lips that kiss not God,

> "There's a wideness in God's mercy,
> Like the wideness of the sea;
> There's a kindness in His justice,
> Which is more than liberty.
>
> . . . .
>
> "For the love of God is broader
> Than the measure of man's mind;
> And the heart of the Eternal
> Is most wonderfully kind."[1]

All of it is true, but we would never have known it if it had not been for Him in whom we have seen the Godhead bodily. When He was born the angels sang, "Glory to God in the highest, and on earth peace, good will toward men."[2] Good will, love, was present when He came. It grew in shape and splendor all the days of His life. It ascended the mount in His teachings, His living, His dying, His rising. For 1900 years it has tried to rise above the clouds of man-made inference and stupidity. It, and it alone, accounts for the fact that heaven is a place without shut doors, night, death, or pain.

Jesus, coming forth from God, lived the love-life because He above all men knew that "God is love."

John taught saying, "Beloved, let us love one another: for love is of God; and every one that loveth is born of God, and knoweth God. He that loveth not knoweth not God; for God is love."[3] Such concepts were not born out of the dusty paths of ordinary human events. They were born out of a companionship, companionship with Jesus.

Paul penned the greatest hymn of love ever written, not because he was the world's great lover, but because he knew the world's great lover, even Jesus.

What could be said of Jesus as He stood at the tomb of Lazarus could be said of Him at any of the thousand milestones of human experience, "Behold how he loved him!"[4]

Jesus could sing the praises of love because He knew God intimately who "is love." Paul and John could sing of love because they knew Jesus who manifested a radiant good will toward man and God. And Jesus and Paul and John loved others, touching them with the magic wand of Christian affection, because all three knew the highest wisdom of the race, "He that loveth not knoweth not God; for God is love."[5]

Ted Malone once observed that "there is nothing so empty as an empty mail box" and then quoted Mary Carolyn Davies' lovely quatrain,

> "Not snow nor sleet nor cold nor heat,
> Can ever quite prevail,
> To stop small bits of paradise
> Coming through the mail!"[6]

Surely all of us during our years on earth have been conscious of these "small bits of paradise" that have come to us from God, reminding us that we must not only believe in love, but that we must love! As Jesus expressed it, "Thou *shalt* love."

I BELIEVE IN LOVE BECAUSE I AM SELFISH

The tears and the smiles of the years have taught me that love is the strongest building force in the entire world. Hate warps. Envy corrodes. Greed corrupts. Jealousy distorts. Bitterness shrinks. Evil decays. The little spites of life are in reality termites eating away the foundations of our happiness. The little sins we enjoy are but the teeth of the saw with which we cut through the limb that holds us to the tree of life. To hate, to envy, to be greedy and jealous, wanton and morally careless, means that we are destroying life as surely as if we took poison, which in fact we are actually taking. These traits slowly but surely decrease our stature and destroy the soul.

All of us know these things. We know that we are our best and truest selves when affectionate good will warms our hearts and goes forth in a healing glow to touch the lives of others. It heals life's hurts. It straightens and strengthens. It cleanses and corrects. It stabilizes and establishes. It transforms death into life, sorrow into gladness, defeat into victory, and draws all of us nearer to one another and nearer to God. Love builds and beautifies, and therefore I believe in love.

I BELIEVE IN LOVE BECAUSE IT TEACHES ME WHAT OUGHT TO BE!

Love is never satisfied with what it is. There is in it an urge toward perfection. That is why Jesus said, "You . . . must be perfect, as your heavenly Father is perfect."[7] We must not permit ourselves to be content with what is bad when we can make it good. We must not be satisfied with the good if it can be made better, and we must not rest until we have done all in our power to raise "the better" to the superlative "best."

He who knows love as "eros" limits love to the animal kingdom. This is but the love of the body. He who knows love as "philia" knows the higher love of friendship, love for those we like and who love us. He who knows love as "agape" knows the love with which Jesus loves humanity. The world needed His love and therefore He loved. Our word charity carries in its heart the same concept, for to the Hebrew the word charity (*zedakah*) means "right doing," "righteousness."[8] Surely Christianity must not descend to a lower level. Surely we must adhere to the admonition of John, "Beloved, if God so loved us, we ought also to love one another."[9]

Therefore we must not enjoy our hates! We must not thrill to the intoxication of greed and jealousy, envy and vengeance. Our prejudices must not be stronger than our principles, nor our vices than our virtues.

Love, as Jesus and John knew it, was no "blind impulse," no emotional spree. It was a building social force, a controlling force, a wisdom that taught that our days and years are not ladders and staircases of convenience whereby we descend into hell, but rather ladders and staircases whereby we ascend to heaven. If "love is of God" then life must ascend! If religion is or ought to be God's philosophy of life wherein love is the most active principle, then Christianity should be above all else the manifestation of love, between man and God, man and man! Surely Jesus had this very thought in mind when He said that all the commandments are epitomized in two: "Thou shalt love the Lord thy God . . . And . . . thy neighbour as thyself."[10] And John follows after with the conviction that if we do not love the people we see how can we say we love God whom we do not and cannot see?

The greatest sin of the world, the greatest sin of Christendom, is lovelessness, our lack of a spirit of good will toward others. To love those who love us, said Jesus, is paganism. That has always been the rule of the jungle! But to love those who are unlovely, to love those who misunderstand and hurt us, that is to be Christian! So firmly was Jesus convinced of it that He prayed forgiveness from the cross upon those who drove the nails, and in His death promised personal companionship to a dying convict.

I remember one summer afternoon when a little boy of eight strode toward my car preparatory to going home. I noticed that he held a big fat toad in each hand, and that his overall pockets were bulging. With skillful argument I persuaded him to let the toads go, and then I asked him what he had in his pockets. He looked startled, then embarrassed, and slowly took from his little pockets, six other toads, and tearfully left them in the grass.

Adults will never understand why little boys like to fill their pockets with toads. To adult eyes they are ugly and slimy. I sometimes think that we must look pretty much like toads to God, and yet He loves us. And why? Is it not because God knows that only by love can godly character be built? Is it not because He is dissatisfied with what is and works for that which ought to be? Is it not because, being God, He cannot be satisfied with anything save the best?

I BELIEVE IN LOVE, AND I DO SO BECAUSE INTELLIGENT LOVE IS A DAILY NECESSITY

What a price we pay for unintelligent love! Think of the warped personalities, the weakened wills, the unhappy people and homes, that result from love that is not love. When God fashioned the human body He placed our heads above our hearts, and by that physiological fact, God is ever saying to us, "Make your love intelligent." The head is supposed to control our love so that we are not foolish. Our hearts are supposed to warm and control our heads lest they be cold and brutal. Heads and hearts should work in partnership!

Is not that one of the needs of today? Many of our ministers, teachers, and politicians are people with good hearts and soft heads. They have not learned that to love is not enough. We must love with intelligence. To give a bottle of milk a day to every child in the world would be a very fine thing, but is it practicable? To feed all the hungry of the world is an admirable desire, but is it within reason? To do business with Russia would be a blessing to mankind, but who can do business with Russia? To desire to do good, to desire to get along with others, is admirable, but our good will, our social love, must be intelligent. Love wrongly used can be as destructive as hate!

It would be wonderful to find and follow a system of economics and government that would rid the world of poverty and disease, backbreaking labor and tedious routine, injustices and moral blemishes. If socialism and communism could actually accomplish such a goal I would join them before sunset. But no system, save the system of love, can ever rid the world of the things that separate man from man, and man from God. Is such a system possible and practical? God thinks so! That is why Jesus came! That is what Christianity is supposed to accomplish! Christianity is supposed to be love in action in society!

Christianity is the religion of love. Christians are supposed to be the people who love as God loves. Christians are supposed to make love the outstanding characteristic of personality and conduct. By the love we bear to those who share with us life's way we either manifest or deny our love for God.

Love, intelligent Christian love, ought to make us socially conscious. Love ought to open our eyes to injustices and wrongs in the little world of our community, and in the larger realm of the earth! It should not blind us to slums in people or people in slums. It should rather trouble us that we live day after day as calloused as a field hand's foot. John has said, "Whoso hath this world's good, and seeth his brother have need, and shutteth up his heart of compassion against him, how dwelleth the love of God in him?"[11] He also said, "If a man say, I love God, and hateth his brother, he is a liar."[12]

Love to be intelligent must not be a vague love for the unseen God. It must be a vital love for visible people. And we who are the disciples of Christ, and therefore the devotees of love, must make that love known by our concern for the welfare of others. We must not only love those who love us, we must learn to have good will toward those who do not love us, nay, even to those who are our enemies.

I BELIEVE IN LOVE BECAUSE ONLY BY LOVE CAN I BECOME A SON OF GOD

Is not the world weary of hearing us smugly say that to be a Christian we must believe this and that about God and Christ? Has not the time come when we must put the emphasis on love in action? For centuries we have cried "credo" when God was trying to teach us to say "amo."

Suppose you check the following characteristics of love as set forth by Paul in the thirteenth chapter of First Corinthians:

1. Are you patient?
2. Are you kind?

3. Are you contented with your lot in life?
4. Are you humble?
5. Are you thoughtful of others, especially people you do not know and may never see again? Are you thoughtful of your cook, your maid, the yardman, the clerk in the store, the driver on the bus, the operator of the elevator, the Negro who has to push his way through an aisle of white folks in order to reach the rear of the bus, the fellow who bumps against you on the sidewalk?
6. Are you unselfish?
7. Are you emotionally controlled, keeping your temper a secret?
8. Are you willing to give the other fellow the benefit of the doubt?
9. Are you consciously trying to see yourself and others in terms of God and not merely in terms of social customs?

Are you persuaded that love and love alone can

1. Make life courageous?
2. Make life secure?
3. Make life interesting and vital?
4. Make life cheerful and understanding?
5. Make life wholesome?
6. Make life meaningful?
7. Make life beautiful?
8. Make life eternal?

If God is love, then Christ is God's love letter to the world, God's Valentine! Christ is God's invitation to you and to me to become better people, eternal people. If in this world we become like the things and people we love, then does it not stand to reason that in the life to be we shall be like the things and people we love? If in this life we love the godly shall we not dwell with the godly hereafter? If in this life we love the ungodly, shall we not go on loving the ungodly beyond the grave?

It was not by shallow thinking that Paul affirms that love is better than eloquence, better than prophetic foresight, better than miracle-working faith, better than generosity, and better than martyrdom. Nor was it by chance that he concluded his great dissertation on love with the words, "And now abideth faith, hope, love, these three; but the greatest of these is love."

If I want to live forever in the presence of God I must learn to love, not merely God, but people. Not merely the people I like, but the people I do not like at all.

I have often thought that it is fear that makes us less than Christian. Fear seems to be basic in selfishness, greed, covetousness, envy, and all immorality. Many prejudices receive our allegiance, not because we feel they are right and justifiable, but because we fear the consequences if we go against the accepted mores.

And how shall one rise above his bad prejudices and be true to his good ones? How shall one cease to be selfish, greedy, covetous, envious, and immoral? By getting rid of the fear that undergirds these traits. And how shall one do that? John says that only love can "cast out fear"; only God's love for us, and only our love for one another.

Christianity is best affirmed in its practical results rather than in its theological subtleties. Jesus cut through all the red tape of churchism when He said to Peter, "Peter, do you love me?" "If you love me take care of my lambs, take care of my sheep."

I have not forgotten the old Welshman who was bitterly criticized by the church people in his community because he seldom went to church. He was a congenial, quiet man, who loved people, and also loved a fishing trip. One Sunday morning he entered the village just as the people were returning from divine worship. "Well," said one of the elders, "so you have missed kirk again. So you have again been wasting your time in the field when you should have been under God's roof. What have you to say for yourself?" "Only this," replied the man, "I have just taken a few fish to three families who are being starved to death because of the high rent you are charging them."

Oh, my friends, *love is the final test of Christianity.* You may be able to recite the Creed faultlessly. You may know every answer to every catechetical question. You may know the books of the Bible, and much contained within them. But if you do not love people, if you cannot live with a spirit of good will toward all men, you have not even touched the hem of Christ's garment, let alone touched His sacred hands.

Is it not a shame that you and I live out our days with our skins filled with little hates and sins, when God wants us to be filled with good will toward men? Is it not a sin for us to ask that God be understanding of us, forgiving and merciful, when we spend so much of our time stabbing people in the back, cutting their throats, dirtying their names, and defaming their character?

If we do not learn to live with increasing love within our hearts for others, how shall we ever gain heaven and enjoy the haven of God's care?

Let us not live as if we are saying, "I believe in love, but . . .," but rather as if we were taking seriously the commandment of Christ and of John, "God is love; therefore, love."

CHAPTER FOUR

"I Believe in Loyalty, But..."

(MARK 11:1-11)

ತಾ

LOYALTY is that quality which moves a man to be true to a trust when he could, by rationalizing, evade it. Loyalty is enthusiastic allegiance. When a person is faithful to a cause or a person at risk and sacrifice to himself we say he is loyal.

JESUS WAS LOYAL TO THE HIGHEST

The triumphal entry into Jerusalem is a study in loyalty, and the one clear lesson is this: Christians, like Jesus Christ, ought to be loyal to the highest.

Not many Christians are! We habitually condition our loyalties to the things we want to do rather than to the things we ought to do. Life for most of us is a watering-down process whereby our loyalties are limited to the persons and causes we can handle without too great cost to ourselves. It seems to be human nature to seek out and find reasons for breaking those ties of life that demand great loyalty and great sacrifice.

Very few of us are loyal to the best within ourselves. We seldom rise to the best we know. We compromise, we lower, we rationalize, we do all we can to arrange relationships so that we can appear to be giving our best when actually we are making little more than a token gesture.

Thus lip service becomes characteristic of most Christians. We talk faith, courage, hope, and love. We seem to have a profound respect for God and things religious, but what we are inside, what we live, or what we express in our living, is a distant relative to the religion of Jesus. Hence most of us are more loyal to our prejudices than we are to our principles, more faithful to our advantages than to our obligations. We talk a wonderful religion but we live a very mediocre one.

It was so on that first Palm Sunday. The friends of Jesus were enthusiastic that day. They tore branches from the trees and scattered them in the streets. They wanted Jesus to know how loyal they were to Him personally, and to the Kingdom He was soon to establish.

Of course, they did not own the trees they denuded. The trees belonged to someone else. I wonder what the city officials thought? I wonder what the owners of private property said? Suppose this crowd had passed your house, tearing up your shrubs and trees? Doubtless the crowd reasoned that Jesus would soon be king and could then sign an order replacing the trees at public expense. Or did they think at all?

They also took off their cloaks and cast them in the street as a symbol of their allegiance and devotion. How easily we cast before Jesus the things that do not matter! Has not the word, "rummage," become part of Christianity? Is it not our usual procedure to give our cast-off garments as a symbol of our Christian concern? Do not all of us give a few dollars there and here to help the needy and the underprivileged and think we are doing Christian social service work? We are trained to give to Christ what we do not need, and to keep all else.

Yes, they cast their garments before Him. But He wanted their hearts and their lives, not their garments. He came seeking people who by high ideals and right living would re-shape the world to God's intent, and all He received were branches from someone else's trees and garments that were for a moment spread in the street. They did not give themselves, and what they gave cost them nothing.

Had I been on the little donkey that day I would have been flattered by the acclaim. I would have smiled and bowed to left and right, and waved to all. But someone in the crowd would doubtless have said of me what an aged colored woman said about Mr. Roosevelt when he visited Asheville some years ago. She had stood for hours to see the great President of the United States, and when she saw him, she shook her head and said, "Pshaw, he is only a man."

He who rode the little donkey was more than a man. That is what makes this Palm Sunday procession the most pathetic of all Scriptural stories. Jesus gave up heaven to save man. He lived out His life in dire loneliness. He was the recipient of man's inhumanity and arrogance. He lived a perfect life and had done all He could to help man see the beauty and the value of the "good." Ahead of Him was the stark cross, its cold shadow already black upon the streets of the ancient city. He was riding to His death, thus making complete His willingness to do everything for man's salvation, and in return for all His sacrifice and loyalty He got branches torn from someone else's trees, and garments cast in the dust of the street. He was giving everything He had. They gave as little as they could.

If I had been in His place that day I would have jerked the tiny donkey to the side. I would have told the crowd what I thought of their loyalty and sacrifice. I would have turned the little beast about and would have ridden angrily out of the city and back to the loneliness of Olivet. I would have let them know that I would not waste another hour on such people, and hence there would be no Holy Communion, no

Good Friday, and no Easter joy. "Man," I would have shouted, "is not worth saving."

You would have understood, would you not? When a man has given his best for others, and all he gets is empty words and actions, there is no reason why he should throw his life away, casting divine pearls before human swine. You who never like inconveniences and expensive loyalties, you would understand, wouldn't you?

I do not know the thoughts of the Son of God as He rode that triumphant way which had no victory, a way as devoid of triumph as the trees were of branches. Yet, He did not turn back. That is what astounds me. He saw their shallowness, their superficiality, their cheap show of loyalty, and still He rode on to die for them. He had set before Himself a responsibility and there was no turning back. He had set out to save man in spite of man and He would be loyal to the highest.

How silly this scene must have seemed to the disciples years later. How embarrassed they must have been as they recalled the mutilated trees. How ashamed of their self-centeredness, their self-seeking, and their selfishness. It would seem to me that every time any one of them touched the robe he had flung in the street he must needs burst into tears. Before Christ's loyalty their heads must have bowed.

JESUS WAS LOYAL TO THE LOWEST

Not only was Christ loyal to the highest, but to the lowest. Being loyal to the lowest is the test of a man's true worth, a man's real self. Jesus came to love the pauper and not merely the prince, the sick and not merely the well, the poor and not merely the rich, the sinful and not merely the righteous. He was willing to stoop to hell itself in order to save a man, and

He never felt unclean in doing so. He was never class-conscious, race-conscious, or place-conscious. He came to save all.

Palm Sunday will be different for me henceforth because I rode a bus from Asheville to Knoxville. I prefer Pullmans and planes, but in order to make connections and get home in a reasonable period of time I rode a bus, and few Pullmans and planes could be as modern and attractive.

My first reaction to a bus trip was irritation, and when I saw the sailors and marines, the farm people and the laborers, not to mention the drunken old codger from Knoxville, I was almost rebellious. As we left Asheville and emerged into the awakening countryside, I was trying to rethink my Palm Sunday message, but the drunk across the aisle kept asking me questions. I tried to be civil, but rapidly reached the place where I wanted to push him back into a corner and tell him to "shut up." Then there was the couple behind me who were discussing world affairs without any knowledge of world affairs. Behind them were some marines who were striving arduously to get the attention of the two girls across the bus. A few colored people sat quietly on the rear seat, and nearer me sat a carpenter from Valdese, with a spirit level in one hand and a bunch of flowers in the other. He and his wife were visiting relatives at Canton. He was in a wonderfully pleasant mood. He said he had looked in the stores of Charlotte and Salisbury for a level and had finally located one in Asheville. It was truly a lucky day for him! And the flowers! Weren't they pretty? Cost ten cents apiece, and were worth it! Why, his wife would rather have a bunch of pretty flowers than a new dress.

Suddenly God illuminated my poor heart. These were Palm Sunday people. They were like the people who shouted in the streets, tore branches from the trees, and cast down their garments before Christ. These were the kind of people made immortal by Charles Dickens, real people, people for whom Jesus lived and died. God loved these fellow passengers as much as He loved anyone. They, too, were His children.

I listened and looked with new interest. They were much more interesting than the seasonal escapists I had seen in Asheville hotels, people who spent their years running after good weather and running away from their boresome selves. These people at least worked and produced. They were making a real contribution to a stable country. Of course I liked the escapists because they were attractive and clean. They spoke good English and knew books and places, but these people were closer to real life and formed the strong backbone of church, state, and world.

I looked at the carpenter from Valdese. For forty-three years he had built houses and barns. He talked of his buildings as if they were his children. He felt he had contributed something to mankind and the nation. His saw and hammer had left a constructive mark on America, and his spirit level had built straightness into life.

"Jesus was a carpenter," I said to myself. "If this were the year 30 or 33 A.D. and someone had come to me saying, 'Come and see the carpenter from Valdese,' would I have gone? If such a man came upon the horizon today would I listen to him, a carpenter from a small town in the hills? Are not carpenters people we hire at so much an hour? How could a carpenter have the words of eternal life? Would any respectable church leader invite the carpenter from Valdese to his home for a holiday week end? Would he be likely to become the follower of a carpenter from Valdese?"

That is the way I talked to myself on the bus. I also said to myself, "I wonder if I would have liked Christ's disciples?"

What could one say in front of a carpenter from Valdese who had as his followers a group of fishermen from the waterfronts of Charleston and Savannah? How many of us would be happy over admitting Matthew, the grafting servant of the Roman lords, into church membership? How many would introduce Mary Magdalene to sons and daughters — and husbands? How many would pause before the mountain woman standing on the corner and say, "O mother of Jesus, mother of us all, we pause to express to you our love and admiration?" Do you think you would like to have that mountain woman as your guest at noon today?

Sitting there on the bus I suddenly realized that these were the real Gospel characters, the drunk and all! These were the real people of Palm Sunday. These were the people who followed Jesus and heard Him gladly. These were the same, except the others were Jews!

I would never have attempted to do what God did. Nor would you. If we were to set out to establish a Kingdom in the world we would strive to secure our leaders from the elite. Yet God chose a carpenter from Nazareth, some fishermen from the waterfronts of Galilee, and ordinary people from the farms and industries of the countryside. Did He do it in order to impress upon us that God can take the lowest and make it the highest? Was Jesus thus saying that God loves all and can transform the ordinary into the extraordinary, and make His saints from lowly sinners? The Jews believed that prosperity was the highest sign of God's favor, but Jesus said that God has no favorites. He loves all men.

That is how our Christianity began. It began with a carpenter, some fishermen, and a crowd of ordinary people. That is how Christian democracy was born. That is how America was born. That is why Christianity at its best, Christ's kind of Christianity, is the highest religion in the world.

Before I reached Knoxville, I was aglow with a new spirit. Jesus seemed to be on the bus as we drove over the Great Smokies, mountains of green timber carpeted with snow. It seemed to me that I was riding with the Jesus people, the people of the Gospels and the New Testament, and I felt the presence of Him who taught and loved the multitudes.

Jesus was loyal to the very lowest because He was loyal to the very highest, and the reason why we are disloyal to the lowest is because we are also disloyal to the highest. One of the unfortunate circumstances of life is that most of us in modern churches never have a fair opportunity of seeing these interesting people who make up the larger portion of the race. Oh, we see them in shops and on streets, but we do not know them at all, and because we do not know them in their needs and their battles, their defeats and victories, we are prone to forget that Christ loved them very, very much, and it was from their ranks that He called His disciples and His friends.

JESUS WAS LOYAL TO THE FULLEST

Not only was Jesus loyal to the highest and to the lowest, He was loyal to the fullest. He was the only man who could come to life's end feeling that "it is finished."

I once heard John Timothy Stone say that "an excuse is a statement of the circumstances under which a man fails to do his duty." What statement do we make? I know what mine is, but when Palm Sunday dawns and brings into being another Holy Week with all its rich and enriching glory, I am a man without excuses.

This I know: Jesus gave everything He had for the salvation of the world, and most of us have given branches torn from someone else's trees and have made a gesture by casting old garments before Him!

During the last century the Church might have evangelized the nation and the world. The opportunity was ours. We had the men and the money. We had the truth in Holy Writ and the spiritual resources. What were we thinking about all that time?

The War Between the States would never have occurred if we had been true to the New Testament. The Spanish-American War would not be part of history today. The two great World Wars which have broken the British Empire, corrupted the whole earth, and compelled us to sink or swim in the troubled waters of this era, need never have happened. We could have tried Christ's way and Christ's methods and built thereby the Parliament of Man and the Congress of Peace. Instead our land and our world is a place of terror, terror born of our disloyalty to God, our refusal to be loyal to the highest and the lowest.

Dr. Ralph Sockman has a very interesting sermon entitled, "Trifling with the Eternal,"[1] He has called our attention to the story Jesus told of the royal feast to which the aristocracy of the realm was invited, but the privileged, the invited guests, made light of the invitation, and did nothing. Some looked after their estates. Others had to hurry away to close a business deal. Others were engrossed in the affairs of home. The king sent out his messengers a second time, and with the same result. The privileged took lightly the king's invitation. They all had excuses as to why they could not attend. The story closed by the king's sending forth his armies and destroying the city and the privileged and bringing in instead the common people from the highways and hedges.

Dr. Sockman says that God always extends His invitations to the privileged first, but when they do nothing about it, when they take Him lightly, the world knows the power of the mob, the power of the military, and the destruction of war.

We could have built a better world during the last century, but we were too busy with other things. We would not give our sons to the cause, and our government has sent them forth to the ends of the world. We would not give our money, and the government has taken it from us in abundance. We have been penny-wise and dollar-foolish. We have been business-wise and spiritually foolish. Too many of our loyalties have been of the Palm Sunday variety, branches from someone else's trees, and our garments cast in the street, and a period of emotionalism which ended in our doing nothing about the things of God.

How long, how long before we learn that we cannot trifle with God and prosper? How long dare we treat lightly His invitations? How long will we take care of our business and ignore His? How long before we learn that there is no material prosperity apart from moral and spiritual vitality? How long before we see clearly that only by being loyal to the highest can we have prosperity and peace?

We are living in the Noah days of history, days that may well precede the rise of the communistic waters that are threatening to deluge the entire earth, wiping out the world we know, leaving only a remnant of believers which shall be seed in the hand of God for the rebuilding of a nobler race. And all because you and I, our fathers and our grandfathers, have continually said, "Yes, I believe in God, I believe in loyalty to God, but . . . ."

CHAPTER FIVE

"I Believe in God, But . . ."

(GENESIS 28:10-19)

ह≈

MY PURPOSE is not to attempt to prove the existence or personality of God, for I can no more prove God than I can prove
that a flower is pretty, a scene majestic, a baby innocent, or
an elderly person wonderfully sweet. There are some things
I must decide on the basis of my own rational and emotional
reaction to life, and it is thus I accept God. The Bible does
not argue about Him, nor did Jesus; why should I? It is no
great feat to outline and discuss the rational arguments for belief in God, and they have their place in theology, but my
purpose is not argument.

No one realizes better than I the temperament of modern
man concerning theology. He has voted it out of existence.
He feels he has killed it with the dagger of intellect, the club
of doubt, and the jujitsu of modern psychology. He will
tell you that he is not interested in theology.

But can man escape theology? He may vote the theology
of other generations and other people out of his life. He may
kill the thoughts of this theology or that, but in the end he
himself must decide what he believes about God, either as a
theist or an atheist, and in that moment he builds theology
anew. Man can never outlive the restlessness of his soul for
the Divine. He may run away as did Jacob, leaving behind
familiar faces and places, but he will soon discover that his
new non-theistic hiding place is also the place of God.

Jacob's dream suggests three of the fundamental characteristics of true theology.

THEOLOGY MUST CONCERN ITSELF WITH A REVELATION

Theology, in order to be something more than philosophy,
must concern itself with a revelation from above. "Christian
doctrine agrees that there is no experience of God without a
revelation from God."[1] Theology must concern a ladder, let
down from heaven, a golden ladder whereby man may ascend
from his hell to his Paradise, a ladder freely given of God but
arduously used by man.

Christianity is such a ladder, and it is here that we lay claim
to its being a unique religion. The revelation of which Christianity speaks results from the normal intercourse between the
human and the divine; God speaks or reveals Himself through
persons in such a way as to emphasize the spiritual qualities
of human nature and their larger uses in the hands of God.
We do not speak of ready-made religious books dropped from
above or hidden in nearby hills. We do not talk of trances
and seances. The men through whom God speaks in Christianity are people of spiritual quality, persons of enlarged
souls, persons with expanded spiritual capacities. They are
God's men, and they are good men. Their lives are in keeping with their sacred purposes.

There is a vast difference between the revelation of God in
Christianity and in other religions. Ours concerns a ladder,
but theirs concerns stilts. The stilts help them to walk a little
above the common earth and see a bit farther into tomorrow,
but at best the revelation is shallow and limited. Their out-
stretched arms never lay hold on God as do the hands of John
and Paul. They never find anything save the hem of the
divine garment. Their observations in the realms of nature

and human nature are never transcendent in the larger, purer ways of Christ, and their conclusions are usually of man seeking rather than of God revealing. In them we find intimations of the true God. In them we find aspirations after reconciliation and peace. But only in Christianity does God stand forth clear and beautiful, and only here do we find invitations to great faith, and in it all God is our inspiration and our guide.

Let me hasten to say, however, that I do not mean to suggest that non-Christian peoples have not found God. That would be absurd. Every religion, be it simple or complex, contains truth concerning God and man. There is much that is lovely and true and rich in the great religions of the earth which are not Christian. My contention is not that the others do not speak of the true God, not that they have not found certain truths concerning Him, but that they possess their diamonds in mud. They possess their truths in the muck of falsehood, and at best they have not found the highest revelation of the Divine.

The non-Christian religions, in many instances, did not begin as religions at all, but as systems of morals and ethics. Their founders did not think of themselves as great religious leaders, e.g., Buddha and Confucius. Others are mixtures of many faiths, such as Mohammedanism which contains Hebrew and Christian elements mingled indiscriminately with Arab concepts. At best, the non-Christian religions represent man's search for God, and are therefore like a man standing on the edge of a marsh looking at the stars across a tumbling sea. The heights are the heights of the eye and the lonely heart, and their circumference is the circumference of the people of the tribe. There is no true universality in them.

One can afford to be generous in appraising the non-Christian religions, for Christianity contains all that is good in them and then surpasses them as spring surpasses winter or the stars the sod, and only in Christianity is true universality found. It is part of our faith, and the experience of our mission work discloses that Christianity lives in all lands as if indigenous.

But it is not on the basis of comparative religions that we claim superiority, but on the divine quality of the New Testament. I am persuaded that if we knew nothing of other religions the New Testament would convince us of the uniqueness of our faith, for our religion is founded on a Person who was believed to be, and believed Himself to be, God's eternal Son; one who spoke with authority as if He was sovereign of all the earth, Creator and Lord. There is in Him, in His words and ways, a supra-human element that will not down. There is about Him a divine radiance that the centuries cannot dim.

Christianity's claim to being a true and final revelation is founded on this Person, Jesus the Christ! He is the golden ladder lowered by God to the earth. He is the One who connects man and God, man and man. The ladder and its theological significance no longer waver in dreams, and the words of God are no longer vague words of the night.

Let no one doubt His humanity, but let no one doubt His deity. He certainly is more than man. He is indeed from above! He came to earth to reveal God to man, and man has never been able to think seriously about Him without thinking of God. As Dr. Whale has said, "The Bible is a monument to the fact that the eternal God has never left Himself without a witness; its whole meaning is disclosed in the fact of the Incarnation; God has spoken to us in His Son."

I tell you reverently that I would rather be Jesus revealing God to mankind than be the greatest statesman, the greatest military leader, the greatest inventor and scientist the world has ever known, for their contributions are temporal and transient, while His is eternal and permanent.

If there be no revelation from above then there is no final faith. If there be no revelation from above then our religion is but a weak framework of guesses. Man by himself can do no more than observe the footprints in the sands, the strokes of the paintbrush on the sunset sky, the cycle of seasons and the circle of the stars, and the million inexplicable occurrences of daily life. He cannot of himself find God.

Only by God's own self-revelation can God be known. As C. S. Lewis observes, you can pick up a stone and examine it and know all there is to be known about it. You can stalk and catch animals and by studying them in their natural habitat, and dissecting them, you can know all there is to be known about them. You can study man. You can catch and possess him, but you will learn nothing important about man unless he speaks and reveals his thoughts. The answer to why he does what he does is to be found in his words. Man, being a person, and not a thing or an animal, is a creature of thought, and only when you know his thoughts can you know him.[2]

If this be true of man, how much more true it is of God. Only as God reveals Himself can we know Him, and we know very little of Him until we know Jesus Christ, for He was God incarnate. Small wonder that John thought of Him as God's Word, for in Him we hear God speaking and find the divine motives.

Nor was Jesus unconscious of His unique presence and purpose. "I am from above,"[3] He said. "He that hath seen me hath seen the Father,"[4] "If ye had known me, ye should have known my Father also."[5] He is indeed the golden ladder from above, man's way of salvation, man's only way of attaining Paradise, and true theology must concern itself with Him. Only when we know Him do we realize the meaning of the words, "Thou shalt have no other gods before me." The old gods will not die in your heart until Christ becomes your God.

THEOLOGY MUST CONCERN ITSELF WITH LIFE NOW

Not only must true theology concern itself with a revelation from God, but that revelation must concern life now, it must represent God as active in our behalf. God must be at once both transcendent and immanent, the object of my faith and the power in my faith, the enthroned One above and the active One beneath. He must forever be the One to whom I pray and yet the One who is ever at my side.

Perhaps that is why our God is a Trinity, for only a trinity can do what God must do in order to meet the demands of the spiritual hungers of man. He must be there, and here, and within, all at the same time.

In Jacob's dream God did not come down; He remained above, He spoke from above. It was His angels who ascended and descended. God must always be above us and beyond us, not in terms of space, but in terms of relationships. The Father must always be there, but the Son must be nearer, and the Holy Spirit must be around us and within us.

I do not know how to illustrate this adequately. If I were God I could make God clear, but being man I can only speak as a man knows God. At least this is true: God must at least be like the sun which, though it remains above and beyond us, yet sends down its electronic angels to heal us and give us life. There could be no life here if the sun came too near, and no life if it departed from us. God must be as active as sunlight, as radium, as life, as death, as yeast, as love. He must be apart and yet be ever ministering to the needs of the world.

There is a certain story which you and I have laughed at, but which causes no amusement when you think of it as Dr. George Buttrick thinks of it.[6] The story concerns a man who looks at his neighbor's fruitful garden and says to him, "God has blessed you in your toil." To which the gardening neighbor replies, "Yes, but you should have seen this patch when God had it alone."

Suppose, however, that the man "had it alone." Suppose there were no sunlight and rain from above, no nourishment in the earth, no pull from above, could man grow anything, even weeds? What could man do without God's participation?

This I have observed: God is always active in my life. My times of loneliness, sorrow, sickness, pain, and adversity have not only convinced me of my limited resources, but of God's unlimited resources. I have learned that the great experiences of life cannot be printed on the pages of a book or flashed on the silver screen or preached from a pulpit; they are for the knowing of God alone. I have learned that Love means my best self going out in appreciation and service to meet another best self seeking me; that Truth is my best mind going out to meet other best minds seeking me; that Faith is my best loyalties and convictions going out to meet other best loyalties and convictions that are seeking me. Whenever my best goes forth with searching hands it finds other hands searching for my own. My love finds love. My mind finds truth. My faith finds conviction. My soul finds service. My self finds God who was walking to meet me. Mysterious it may be — as are all the deep experiences of life — but I am convinced that I must at least do as much as a buried bulb: I must put out my roots, dig deep and anchor there, and lift my life toward heaven above in terms of praying leaves and chaliced soul.

The story of the Bible is the story of God active in man's behalf. It it not the story of a God who remains forever above and beyond us, but of a God who, though He remains above, provides a ladder and sends His angels down to bless and save. Theology must portray God as standing at the top of the golden ladder, but it must not forget the angels ascending and descending.

THEOLOGY MUST CONCERN ITSELF
WITH THE SPIRITUAL STRUGGLE

Theology must not only concern itself with a revelation and God's active interest in our lives, but it must also concern itself with our struggles upward.

Like most of us, Jacob was a thief and a liar and a coward. He lied, he stole, and he ran away. He thought he could outrun God, and by distance silence the voice of conscience. God found him. And what did God do? He placed before Jacob a way out of his predicament and then talked with him. He did not talk to him about his sins. He did not thunder threats of violence to come. He is the same God who stood and forgave a woman taken in adultery, the same God who forgave a thief on a cross, the same who ever speaks to sinners in the earth. Only life can make man ripe for salvation, and until he is ripe he cannot understand, and when he is ripe he understands without the militant anger of God.

Here is religious salesmanship at its best. God is seeking to save Jacob the thief, the liar, and the coward, and how does He do it? He opens heaven, He places a ladder on the earth, and He tells Jacob that He is counting on him to be a true son of God. He challenged the best in Jacob, even as Jesus challenged the best in Peter and Matthew and Zaccheus. Here the love of God is showered down in golden splendor upon the sinner, covering him with a robe of glory even as the father received the son from the far country.

Is that all? Fortunately for us, no! God does not pull us heavenward, He makes us climb. Remember how Jacob labored for Laban? Remember the fears that beset him when he went forth to meet Esau? Remember the wrestling in the darkness? Remember the tears of the old man weeping for his sons Joseph and Benjamin? God provides the ladder, but we must do the climbing.

Let all Christians know that there is no elevator to carry us Godward. There is no fancy hocus-pocus whereby a divine chariot comes to carry us home. God does not change our places of stone into feather beds nor rid us of the problems that beset us. Success on earth, yea, and heaven itself, must be earned in the sweat of one's brow. Paradise can only be regained by the steep ascents of righteousness. Only by brains and brawn, courage and faith, do we ascend at all. God does not save us from sickness and sorrow, adversity and death. He lets us suffer and sorrow and die, for that is the scheme of things. And it need not be a bad way. Jesus has convinced us of the fact, and why should we continually cry to escape that which He endured?

High Christian character is not attained save through knowledge, discipline, sacrifice, and service. The angels ascend and descend to strengthen us and sustain us, but they cannot carry us home as long as life remains within these bodies. When Jesus completed the struggle in the wilderness on the note of victory, then, and only then, did the angels come to minister to Him. He belonged to God, and I am persuaded that believing in God means just that, belonging to God, and whom the Lord loveth He chasteneth.

God is not an easy teacher. No good teacher is ever an easy teacher, for there is no easy way of attainment in any field, and certainly there is none in the moral and spiritual field. The only way to learn is to learn. We must gather our knowledge word by word, sentence by sentence, paragraph by paragraph, page by page, book by book, problem by problem, week by week, year by year, and the process of learning does not end until life ends.

No person is educated when he graduates from college. His degree signifies that he may now commence true learning. One does not secure his education in schools. Schools are where one gathers the materials for securing an education. Graduation means that the materials have been gathered and the graduate may now go forth to organize the materials and use them for the larger learning.

We have taught too many generations of Christians that Jesus has done all that is necessary for salvation, when as a matter of fact, God has merely placed the ladder and spoken. Jesus has done all that is needful to establish the ladder and the words, but Christians must still climb, must still struggle upward to Paradise.

We have also taught too many generations of Christians that the important thing is ideas and ideals, and we have felt our task done when we have talked about these twins of knowledge. We forget, however, that God did not give us ideas and ideals for the purpose of holding discussion groups, but for living. Ideas and ideals in the head are of no value at all. Only when they become operative in living are they significant. That is why morals and ethics and spiritual disciplines are important; they testify to what extent the ideas and ideals have been integrated into living.

Only in terms of morals and ethics can we adequately testify to our faith in God. Only in morals and ethics can we adequately affirm our faith in Christ. Christianity is a way of thinking *and* living, thinking that ends in living! The only way a tree can prove its life is by putting forth leaves and blossoms, leaves and fruit. The only way a plant can prove its life is by sending forth roots and raising itself above the earth in terms of beauty and fruitfulness. The only way a person can adequately manifest his faith in God is by expressing his faith in terms of morals and of spiritual values.

The outstanding characteristic of the Church of Jesus Christ must be faith in God. With the open Bible in our hands and the record of the matchless Christ, "I believe in God." Period! Or better still, exclamation mark.

If the outstanding characteristic of the Church is faith in God, then the main task of the Church must be bringing men to God in terms of God-knowledge, God-consciousness, God-service, and God-likeness.

We must think of the Church as a net held in the hands of God and dipped into the sea of life for the purpose of catching men, and that which is the main task of the net must be the task of every part of the net. Every cord must be sound, tight, and useful. The Church is not a club, a society, a philanthropic organization; it is a net held in the hands of God and dipped into the sea of life. When Jesus said, "I will make you fishers of men," He meant that henceforth the disciples were to be parts of God's net, and so are we!

The Church cannot do its work and attain God's goal as long as members keep saying, "I believe in God, but . . . ." We must learn to say, "I believe." Victorious Christianity is never a matter of double or nothing. It is all or nothing!

Now, if there be no God or if there be a god who is not interested in us, and if there is to be no judgment here or hereafter; if Christ was not God incarnate, the Divine Saviour and Friend of man; if there is no golden ladder and no voice, then all is false and all is vanity; love is a lie and life is only another name for death, and we need not concern ourselves with theology. But can men so believe?

Nathaniel Micklem of Mansfield College, Oxford, has written a poem which sets forth the story of a blind girl who sewed by day and read her Braille Bible each night. As time went on her fingers became calloused and the divine letters were no longer distinguishable. Frantically she sought a way of restoring the sensitive touch to her fingers by paring away the callouses, but she discovered that so great was the pain resulting that she could neither sew nor read. Then came the evening when she raised the Braille Bible to her lips to kiss it farewell before placing it on the shelf, only to discover that her sensitive lips which quivered in sacred sadness were sensitive to the letters and she could kiss the words into life.

For years our calloused hands have troubled us and there have been times of pain and sorrow as we tried to work and worship with success. Too often we have thrown the Holy Word away because we could not read the letters through our callouses. Has not the time come when we must kiss the Word to know its blessing afresh?

Franz Werfel stands out, in my opinion, as the most creative writer of my generation, one who will be remembered when others are silent. In one of his books he says, "In its preoccupation with the old, barren parliamentary geography of Right and Left, the world has forgotten that there is an Above and a Below."[7] Theology concerns the "Above and Below," and as Werfel so skillfully suggests, if a man, even a doubting man, will extend so much as his little finger upward toward God, he may find that his whole hand has been seized and his whole life lifted by the Divine.[8]

CHAPTER SIX

"I Believe in Christ, But..."

(JOHN 1:29-45)

ϑ❧

CHARLES SERGEANT JAGGER, English sculptor, had one great desire, to create a statue of Jesus so lovely that men would be moved to repentance and adoration in its presence. Time after time he made the attempt, and time after time he failed. The radiant touch seemed to evade him until finally he was on the verge of despair. It was then, he says, that Jesus suddenly opened the door of the studio and stood there saying, "Try it again." Jagger did try it again, and the statue he carved stands today at Kelham, England, as a benediction to all who see it.

All my ministry I have been trying to present Christ in all the beauty and winsomeness of His character, and I have never been able to do so. Today I try again, and I must try again and again, until men see Him as I see Him, God's Son, the blessed Saviour, the true source of all our hope and confidence, for only as men behold Him in all the rich splendor of His life will men be reborn into newness, and dedicated to noble Christian living. Everything depends on men seeing Jesus as He is, for our concept of God and man is based on what we think of Christ.

WHAT DID MEN THINK OF CHRIST?

Christ once put this question to the Jews of His day, "What think ye of Christ?"[1] It is a deathless question, and one which every individual and generation must answer. It is one that you must answer. "What think *ye* of Christ?"

Caiaphas, the high priest, having seen and heard Jesus, said to his fellow conspirators, "It is expedient for us, that one man should die for the people, and that the whole nation perish not."[2] He it was who later taught the rabble to cry, "Crucify him, crucify him."

Certain unscrupulous businessmen who used the Temple courts as places of merchandise said, "This man will ruin us. He must go."

His worst enemies said He was possessed by a devil, and by the powers of the chief of devils worked great miracles. It was thus His enemies spoke, and they spoke thus because they feared His leadership, for as He increased they decreased.

With His friends it was otherwise. John the Baptist, having talked privately with Jesus, and therefore knowing the mind of the Master, designated Him as, "the Lamb of God, that taketh away the sin of the world."[3] John the disciple, having lived with Him three or more years, and looking back to those years from the heights of great spiritual insight, said, "The Word became flesh, and dwelt among us (and we beheld his glory, glory as of the only begotten from the Father), full of grace and truth."[4] Andrew, after talking with Jesus for only a short period, ran and found Peter, saying, "We have found the Messiah."[5] Philip, having walked a short distance with the Christ, ran to Nathaniel saying, "We have found him, of whom Moses in the law, and the prophets, did write."[6] Peter, faced with the question, "Whom say ye that I am?" answered, "Thou art the Christ, the Son of the living God."[7] The Samaritan woman at the well ran into the village of Sychar crying, "Come, see a man, which told me all things that ever I did: is not this the Christ?"[8] The soldiers sent to arrest Jesus returned empty-handed, saying, "Never man spake like this man."[9] Even the demons cried out, "Let us alone; what have we to do with thee, thou Jesus of Nazareth? . . . I know thee who thou art, the Holy One of God."[10] Pilate, having examined Him, said, "I find no fault in this man," and washed his hands before the multitude as he added, "I am innocent of the blood of this just person."[11] The centurion who supervised the crucifixion said, "Truly this man was the Son of God."[12] Paul wrote saying that Jesus was "the image of the invisible God, the firstborn of all creation; for in him were all things created . . . and he is before all things, and in him all things consist."[13] Nicodemus, the best of Jews, said, "Rabbi, we know that thou art a teacher come from God."[14]

WHAT DOES MODERN MAN THINK OF CHRIST?

What think ye of Christ? The modern world does not pause long enough to evaluate the Christ. Men pass Him by as if He were not here. Men ignore Him as if He never lived. This is indeed strange, since all that modern man values, all that has lifted him and encouraged him, finds its source in the New Testament. How many in the modern world know Him?

Modern man rejects Jesus as unimportant because He is an exception to their theories. Jesus does not present Himself as the final achievement of an evolutionary process. He is not the fruit of what man calls the "natural." He is supernatural, and the modern world denies the supernatural! It is in order to disprove Christ's deity that men attempt to discount the Fourth Gospel and delete from all others the signs of true divinity. But man will yet learn that, as Emerson said, "The name of Jesus is not so much written as plowed into the history of the world." And one hopes and prays that the day will come to modern man, as it came to Emperor Julian, who, after doing all in his power to restore paganism, finally fell on the battlefield crying to the sky, "O Galilean, Thou hast conquered!"

The modern world has taken the path of least resistance, the path of science and secularism, and hence the broad way that leadeth to destruction. Pagan empiricism is not our best path to a better world of better people. It produced communism. It produced the two most devastating wars in all history. It has produced this day of mad confusion and disorder. It is even now leading us on to a third and final world war. Science is materialistic, and education and sociology based on materialistic science form a trinity of forces that can only end in disintegration. Morals and principles were not born of science nor of sociology. Our Christian morals and ethics spring from God's revelation and are based on divine patterns rather than human. Ignore them we can, but not without imperilling the welfare of the entire race.

Modern man is smart and clever about all things save this, he does not know how to save himself or protect his future. He has forgotten that morality and ethics must follow knowledge as the cars follow a locomotive, and if the cars do not follow in proper order, it means a wreck!

The modern world must do business with Jesus or perish. The modern world must obey Jesus and live, or disobey Him and die. There is no other choice!

WHAT DO I THINK OF CHRIST?

It may be of interest to you to know why I feel as I do about the Christ, and in concluding this meditation I shall attempt to share with you my answer to the question, "What think ye of Christ?"

1. I believe Christ is an authentic historical person. He lived! He is not the fruit of man's imagination. He is not a creature of fiction. He is not the projection of man's desires. He lived. That is the record of the Jewish and Roman historians whose writings we still possess. That is the story of the authenticated Christian writings that have come down to us, some in the Bible and much outside the Bible. On no other ground can we account for B.C. and A.D. On no other ground can we account for the existence of the New Testament, the library of early Christian literature, the millions of copies of later Christian literature, the existence of the Church, and the presence of a cross as the most sacred symbol in the world.

No one who knows the facts doubts the historicity of Christ. They may argue about Him but not about His existence. He lived.

2. I believe in His humanity. He was born. He grew. He ate and drank and slept. He learned and expanded in experience. He was often tired and lonely. He was often happy and singing. He walked with people, talked with them, touched them, and they talked with Him and touched Him. He wept as all men weep, and worked as all men work. He is not like the Christ of Sholem Asch's *The Nazarene,* a man who scarcely touched the earth. He was of the earth, a man! He finally was crucified. He bled, and He died! He was human.

3. I believe He was more than human. I believe He was God. I have studied most of the arguments against man's faith in Christ's deity, and I still believe in His deity. I believe Christ was God incarnate. No other Christ is good enough for me. I need a Saviour, not merely a teacher. I need someone to cleanse my soul of sin and guarantee to me

life beyond death with my Christian loved ones. I need more than a teacher and a good example, for my fault is in my nature, not merely my mind. It was because man believed in the deity of Christ that the evangelists went forth preaching. It was because they believed in His deity that they lived and died, built churches, produced the New Testament, and gave to the world the most wonderful portrait ever drawn. All the great spiritual periods of this land, and of the Western world, have been produced through man's faith in Christ as Saviour. His deity alone can account for the victories of Christianity, and our loss of faith in His deity may well account for our present impotency. If Christ is only another teacher like unto Plato, Socrates, and John Dewey, then we can afford to be indifferent. But if Christ is God incarnate, God come to save us, our only sure path to forgiveness and to God, then we must take Him seriously. It is Christ or chaos!

I am convinced of His deity by His sinlessness. There was no sin in Him. He had no consciousness of sin or sinning, no memory twisted by remorse, no mind and heart bowed down in repentance. Others felt sinful in the presence of His sinlessness. Others confessed their sins to Him, but none ever found sin in Him. For three years His disciples walked with Him and found no sin. For three years His enemies watched Him and found no sin in Him, and in final desperation they hired false witnesses in order to convict Him. The centuries have studied His life and have found no sin in Jesus. He is the only faultless man in all history. He is unique. He has no successors. The more saintly we become the more aware we are of sin in and around us, but Jesus, the most saintly of all, had no consciousness of sin.

Not only was He sinless, but *He claimed the power to forgive sin.* He took upon Himself this characteristic of God. We can ignore sin. We can overlook sin. We can excuse sin. We cannot wipe it out. He claimed power to erase it, "Thy sins be forgiven thee." When time runs out and eternity becomes reality, men shall be judged by the Christ, for only He can forgive. In the end He is to be the ridge that divides humanity, He is to be the difference between the lost and the saved.

I am convinced of His deity by *His claims of authority*. He claimed power over the forces of nature and of human nature, of earth and eternity. He spoke with the authority of God. He claimed authority over all men in all lands in all ages. Horace Bushnell graphically summarized Reinhard's argument for the deity of Christ: "Never having seen a map of the world in His whole life, or heard the names of half the great nations on it, He undertakes, coming out of His shop, a scheme as much vaster and more difficult than that of Alexander as it proposes more; and what is more divinely benevolent! This thought of a universal kingdom cemented in God . . . the rustic tradesman of Galilee propounds even this for His errand, and that in a way of assurance as simple and quiet as if the immense reach of His plan were, in fact, a matter to Him of no consideration."[15]

"Here is an extraordinary thing," says Dr. Robert E. Speer, "that out of the most centripetal race in history, from the environment of a small Syrian village, there should have come one whose view and purpose embraced the whole of humanity."[16]

"Heaven and earth shall pass away," said Jesus, "but my words shall not pass away."[17]

Look at the claims: Light of the World, Water of Life, The Door, The Good Shepherd, The Vine, The Bread from Heaven, The Resurrection and the Life, The Son of God, The

Pre-existing Son, The Messiah, The Sent Redeemer, The Way, the Truth, and the Life, Lord of the Sabbath, Greater than Solomon, Truer than Moses, Comforter of All, Master and Lord, The Eternal One.

Think you a man would say, "All power is given unto me in heaven and in earth. Go ye therefore, and teach all nations, baptizing them in the name of the Father, and of the Son, and of the Holy Ghost: teaching them to observe all things whatsoever I have commanded you: and, lo, I am with you alway, even unto the end of the world"?[18]

I believe in His deity because of *His unique consciousness of oneness with God.* He claimed pre-existence with God. He claimed to be God's special representative. He claimed to speak for God as no prophet dared speak. He claimed to be eternal, possessing power of life and death over men. Men then, and men since, have never been able to know Him without thinking of the Father. "I and my Father are one,"[19] He said; "He that hath seen me hath seen the Father."[20] "I must work the works of him that sent me."[21]

I believe in His deity because of *His consciousness of being the sent Redeemer!* He came to seek and to save the lost. He came to ransom man. He came to be the Lamb of God that taketh away the sin of the world. He was the Suffering Servant of God, the one slain from the foundations of the world. He saw His birth, His life, His death, and His resurrection as part of God's redemptive plan, nay, the whole of it!

Dr. Philip Schaff, prince of Church historians, has written, "The chief positive cause of the rapid spread and ultimate triumph of Christianity is to be found in its own absolute intrinsic worth, as the universal religion of salvation, and in the perfect teaching and example of its divine-human

Founder, who proves Himself to every believing heart a Saviour from sin and a giver of eternal life."[22]

Pliny the Younger, writing to Emperor Trajan in A.D. 100, said of the Christians, "They had been accustomed to assemble on a fixed day before daylight and sing by turns a hymn to Christ as a God." Why to Christ "as a God"? Simply because the apostles and the early Christians believed in Jesus as God, and from the first administered the sacrament of Baptism as the symbol of eternal salvation, and the Lord's Supper as the symbol of the death of the Son of God who died for the sins of man.

The two great teachings of the New Testament are repentance and resurrection: repentance whereby the sinner is reconciled unto God, and resurrection which is the direct result of the saving power of Christ as God.

When I have analyzed all He was, all He said, all He did; when I have read the record of the centuries wherein He has walked, and have evaluated the opinions of men, I come to but one conclusion: Jesus was either all He claimed to be, all He permitted men to believe Him to be, or He was the greatest fraud in all history. If He is a fraud, then He is not even a good man, but a cheat and a liar.

Let no man say, "I believe in God, but not in Christ," for no man knows anything concrete about the character of God or how man ought to live His life before God, save those who have known Christ. In Him, and in Him alone, do we behold God. He was God incarnate!

If Jesus was only a man then we must turn our churches into lodge halls and schoolrooms, for we have no right to worship a man as God. If Jesus was only a man then we as Christians are idolaters. He must cease to have churches dedicated to His name. He must cease to be the object of our worship.

We must tear out and throw away the hymns that speak of Him as deity, and we must delete our libraries of all books and essays that set Him forth as divine Redeemer. We must cease to pray in His name and cease putting His words and example above those of other good and worthy leaders. If He was only a good man, then He cannot cleanse my soul of sin nor guarantee to me life beyond the grave, the two things most essential to my peace and confidence.

If the apostles and early Christians had believed Jesus to be merely a good man, they would never have written the New Testament, produced the Bible, sent out evangelists, erected churches, lived and died for their faith; and as long as Christians are deluded into believing that He was only a man, better than others, but not superior to all, unique and alone in all human history, our Christianity will be a thing of shallow truth and our impact on the world devoid of saving power.

WHAT THINK YE OF CHRIST?

If Christ is what the New Testament declares Him to be, if He is what Paul and the apostles believed Him to be, if He is what the early Church and the historic Church have taught concerning Him, then He is not one to be ignored or treated with indifference or careless minds. He is our only way! He is our only hope!

One last thought I would share with you concerning Christ: He is not dead. The normal posture of a true Christian is not that of looking backwards to a man sitting on a hillside, but out and upward toward a Christ who lives today, who stands at the right hand of God the Father Almighty.

My Christian faith is not in a record 1900 years old. My faith is in One who lives today, knows me, knows my world, and is trying to change things for the better through Christians. The importance of the Record lies in the fact that it tells me what happened 1900 years ago when men walked with Him, and thus assures me that what happened to men then, and to the world through such men, can happen again. Peters can still be produced, and Johns, and Pauls; and a pagan world can again be conquered.

My faith is not in a book nor in a church, but in a living Person. The Book is important because it is my map, and the Church is important because it is my door, but He is important because He is my Lord and Saviour. God has seen fit to educate me through the use of the Book, and so I read it. God has seen fit to designate the Church as His means of saving the world, and so I am a member and a servant of it. But neither the Book nor the Church must shadow Him who alone is the Peace of man's soul and the Shelter of man's destiny.

My personal appraisal of Christ and His exalted place in history is set forth in regal splendor by Dr. Philip Schaff in the following words:

"The first century is the life and light of history and the turning point of the ages. If ever God revealed Himself to man, if ever heaven appeared on earth, it was in the person and work of Jesus of Nazareth. He is, beyond any shadow of doubt, and by the reluctant consent of skeptics and infidels, the wisest of the wise, the purest of the pure, and the mightiest of the mighty. His Cross has become the tree of life to all nations; His teaching is still the highest standard of religious truth; His example the unsurpassed ideal of holiness; the Gospels and Epistles of His Galilean disciples are still the book of books, more powerful than all the classics of human wisdom and genius."[23]

With Edersheim I believe that if Christ is not the Messiah, then the world has never had, nor will ever have, a Messiah. I believe with Augustine that our souls will be forever restless until they rest in Him. I believe with Renan that regardless of what the surprises of the future may be, they will not produce a life superior to the life of Christ. I believe with Middleton Murry that Jesus is "the profoundest teacher, the bravest hero, the most loving man, that this world has ever known."[24] I believe with Dr. Lloyd Douglas that the world is still vitally interested in Him who wore the Robe! I believe with the poet,

> "He is a path, if any be misled;
>   He is a robe, if any naked be;
> If any chance to hunger, He is bread;
>   If any be a bondman, He is free;
>   If any be but weak, how strong is He!
> To dead men life He is, to sick men, health;
> To blind men, sight, and to the needy, wealth;
> A pleasure without loss, a treasure without stealth."[25]

Do you believe it? Dare you still stand before the world and glibly say, "I believe in Christ, but . . ."?

Someone in the near future must write a book entitled, "The Christless Christians." Someone must make clear to the Christians of our day that respectable paganism is not enough, regardless of the fact that it is called "higher education" and "science." Not until the Christless Christians are transformed into the Christ-Christians can the problems of the Church, the community, the nation, and the world be solved as God would have them solved; and as long as they are not solved in God's way, they are not solved at all.

A skeptic and anarchist once walked into a Paris cathedral during the Mass. He stood there in the shadows while the choir sang, "Agnus dei qui tollis peccata mundi" ("Lamb of God, who taketh away the sin of the world"). As the melody melted into the softness of the organ the man began to weep, and he cried, "O God, what a dream. . . . If only He could!"

The testimony of the Church is that He can! That is the only reason why we have churches and Christians. We must be that message. We must so live that we will convince the world that Jesus can save sinners because He has transformed and saved us.

"If there is no new birth into a new kind of life then the New Testament is unintelligible" and the Church is a fraud.[26]

Paul could say, "I live; yet not I, but Christ liveth in me."[27] Those in this generation who say, "I believe in Christ, but..." have not Christ in them.

CHAPTER SEVEN

"I Believe in the Crucifixion, But ..."

(LUKE 23:33-38)

ॐ

ONE OF THE leading ministers of America told this story some years ago and it made a lasting impression on me. It was during his early ministry when he was pastor of a church near a slum area. One night a boy came to the door and said, "My mother wants you to come and help get her in." Thinking that the woman was drunk the minister suggested that they call a policeman, but the boy said, "It's not that. She's sick and she wants you to get her in."

The minister followed the boy to a back room in a gloomy tenement and there met a woman who was dying. "I'm not going to be here long," she said. "Can you get me in?" He knew what she wanted. She wanted him to assure her of forgiveness and heaven. With calm assurance he began to talk of Jesus the wise teacher, Jesus the social worker, Jesus the kindly friend, Jesus the good example of what men ought to be, but the woman stopped him. "That will do me no good now," she said, "I'm dying. I have no time to follow His example here. Tell me how to get in."

Throwing aside the "new" teachings of modern theology he told her of the God who sent His Son into the world to seek and to save sinners. When he came to Calvary the woman put her hand on his arm and with radiant face said,

"That's it. That's what I mean. He's the one to get me in."
Not only did she get in that night, but the minister got in,
and henceforth preached but one stirring message, "Jesus
Christ and Him crucified."

When I say that I believe in the crucifixion I mean I believe that the Cross of Jesus Christ must be forever central
and supreme in the theology and sociology of the Christian
Church.

The great ridge which has split all time, and all events, is
not Bethlehem, but Calvary. Even as Jesus on the cross is the
mature development of Jesus in the cradle, so Calvary is the
mature event which we see in infant form in Bethlehem.
All time is divided, not so much before and after Christ's
cradle, as before and after Christ's cross.

Someone has said that "the Cross is a place where one long
road ends and a new road begins."[1] That is what the Christian Church has been saying for 1,900 years: Life begins at
the foot of the cross! Regardless of what the world believed
prior to Calvary concerning God and man and the way of salvation, since Calvary mankind has been conscious of the
Cross as God's weapon against evil, and man's bridge to God
and goodness. At Calvary a new road did begin!

It is most strange that it should be so. The cross was to
Christ's world what the electric chair is to ours. It was a
method of getting permanently rid of criminals. Think of it!
Think of linking God and an electric chair in a picture of
sacredness! Try to visualize a world wherein electric chairs
become the central symbol of churches. Think of churches
with electric chairs on top of steeples, electric chairs on altars
and Communion tables, electric chairs dangling from the
rosaries of priest and sister! Think of hymns and poems, books
and plays, oratorios and pictures, with but one theme: the

adoration of and perpetuation of an electric chair as the sacred symbol of Christendom.

That is what we have done with the cross. It was but an instrument of a government's system of capital punishment, and the Church has made it the richest symbol of mankind. The instrument of death is now the symbol of life. The instrument of life-destroyed is today the symbol of life-indestructible.

No human mind conjured up this strange relationship of God and a cross! Man would never have dreamed of keeping faith in God alive through an instrument of death. All that God represents stands in antithesis to all that is represented by the criminal's last cradle, the cross! Only God would have attempted anything so novel and daring. Only God could have conceived of making that symbol of horror a symbol of honor.

It was the presence of this symbol of death that astounded the Jew and disgusted the Greek. It was this same symbol that moved George Bernard Shaw to say: "The central superstition of Christianity is the salvation of the world by the gibbet."

Yes, even in this age of steel all Christians bow in humility before a wooden cross. Here Catholic and Protestant are one. Here all races are one. Here all nations and all generations are one. For here we behold God's redeeming love, the love that cleanses man of sin and clothes him with the grace of God. By Christ's Cross we are lifted into heaven. By His Cross the gates are opened never to close again.

THE WORLD BELIEVES

I believe in the Cross because the world believes in it! I stood one day in the great national cemetery at Arlington. There before me were acres of crosses, crosses that marked the graves of men who had died for God and country. I knew the stories of some and guessed the stories of others. I kept asking myself, "Why the cross?" As gently as the breeze that whispered to the dead, God said, "Greater love hath no man than this, that a man lay down his life for his friends."[2]

The world has made the cross the highest symbol of sacrifice and proudly places it above all the graves of those who have died in the service of this country.

I remember the first time I saw a cross attached to the license plate of a car. "What does that mean?" I asked a friend. "That cross means that the car belongs to a medical man," he replied.

A year or so later a friend of mine graduated from the Presbyterian Hospital in New York and became a nurse. When I saw her pin I noticed that it bore on its surface a familiar symbol, the symbol of the cross. Why the cross? In the years that have followed I have become familiar with one of the greatest social service agencies in the world, the Red Cross. Why the cross? Always familiar words return, "The Son of man came not to be ministered unto, but to minister, and to give his life a ransom for many."[3] The world has made the Cross of Christ the symbol of humanitarian service.

Yes, the world believes in the Cross! The world remembers and will never forget the One who went about doing good, and who unselfishly served the needs of His fellow men.

THE CHURCH BELIEVES

I believe in the Cross because the Church believes in it. Dr. Clarence Macartney relates that once when he was touring Italy he visited a Waldensian chapel in Florence. Over the pulpit was a huge cross. When he asked the pastor why they had placed the cross over the pulpit the man replied, "We have put the cross there in order to let the people know that this is a Christian Church."[4]

From the day of the first Christian Pentecost until now the Cross has been central in the preaching and program of the Church. In the first Christian sermon we find these words, *"Ye men of Israel, hear these words; Jesus of Nazareth, a man approved of God among you by miracles and wonders and signs, which God did by him in the midst of you, as ye yourselves also know: him, being delivered by the determinate counsel and foreknowledge of God, ye have taken, and by wicked hands have crucified and slain."*[5]

From that day on, the Cross was central in the message of the Church. One-fifth of the Gospel of Matthew concerns the death of Christ; two-fifths of Mark; one-fourth of Luke; and one-half of John. *Every letter of Paul is rich in the message of the Cross.* Everywhere he went, Paul said, "I determined not to know any thing among you, save Jesus Christ, and him crucified."[6] "God commendeth his love toward us, in that, while we were yet sinners, Christ died for us."[7] "The wages of sin is death; but the gift of God is eternal life through Jesus Christ our Lord."[8] "For Christ sent me not to baptize, but to preach the gospel: not with wisdom of words, lest the cross of Christ should be made of none effect. For the preaching of the cross is to them that perish foolishness; but unto us which are saved it is the power of God."[9] "We preach Christ crucified, unto the Jews a stumblingblock, and unto the Greeks foolishness; but unto them which are called, both Jews and Greeks, Christ the power of God, and the wisdom of God."[10] "I am crucified with Christ: nevertheless I live; yet not I, but Christ liveth in me: and the life which I now live in the flesh I live by the faith of the Son of God, who loved me, and gave himself for me."[11] "Let this mind be in you, which was also in Christ Jesus: who, being in the form of God, thought it not robbery to be equal with God: but made himself of no reputation, and took upon him the form of a servant, and was made in the likeness of men: and being found in fashion as a man, he humbled himself, and became obedient unto death, even the death of the cross."[12]

In Peter's first letter we read, "Ye were not redeemed with corruptible things, as silver and gold . . . but with the precious blood of Christ, as of a lamb without blemish and without spot."[13] And again, Christ "his own self bare our sins in his own body on the tree, that we, being dead to sins, should live unto righteousness: by whose stripes ye were healed."[14]

From the lips of John we hear these words, "If we walk in the light, as he is in the light, we have fellowship one with another, and the blood of Jesus Christ his Son cleanseth us from all sin."[15]

And John, seeing into heaven, tells us, "I beheld, and I heard the voice of many angels round about the throne and the beasts and the elders: and the number of them was ten thousand times ten thousand, and thousands of thousands; saying with a loud voice, Worthy is the Lamb that was slain to receive power, and riches, and wisdom, and strength, and honour, and glory, and blessing."[16]

Christians carried the sign of the cross across ancient Europe, painting it upon doors and walls, fashioning it for their places of worship and love, making it central in picture and story. Constantine placed it on the Christian flag and the Church placed it on every altar. Missionaries from England, Scotland, and Ireland carried it triumphantly through the dark forests of the continent, and returned it to the homeland crowned with new laurels of Christ's power to save even unto the uttermost.

The Church has made the Cross the central theme of prayer and song, sermon and service. It wrote it deeply into its oldest creed, "Was crucified, dead, and buried."

That was enough for Christians for more than a thousand years. Not until the Council of Trent and the Protestant Reformation did the Church strive to screen the opinions of her great teachers and formulate a definite doctrine. And a screening was needed! The New Testament was buried beneath twelve centuries of superstition and fancy which prevented men from seeing the Cross in its full significance and glory. If it had not been for Protestantism the Cross would still be buried and its supreme meaning unknown. Jesus would have remained a dead figure on a dead tree.

Throughout the Roman Catholic period the Church was more interested in the fact of Christ's death than in a true New Testament theory of His death. Now we have many theories, and constantly stand in danger of forgetting the fact. Nothing is more important than that we rediscover the meaning of the words, "was crucified."

CHRIST BELIEVES

I believe in the Cross because Christ believed in it. Life for Him meant setting His face steadfastly toward Jerusalem, and Jerusalem became the symbol of His divine death. Much of His teaching is given over to His death, and again and again the word "cross" appears in His dissertations. He did all in His power to prepare the disciples for His crucifixion and death, and stated that it was for the purpose of dying that He came into the world.

We see it clearly in His words, "I am the good shepherd: the good shepherd giveth his life for the sheep. . . . As the Father knoweth me, even so know I the Father: and I lay down my life for the sheep. . . . No man taketh it from me, but I lay it down of myself. I have power to lay it down, and I have power to take it again."[17]

We see it best of all in the Lord's Supper. Here above all else is the highest symbol of His love and death. Hear again the words of Paul, "I have received of the Lord that which also I delivered unto you, That the Lord Jesus the same night in which he was betrayed took bread: and when he had given thanks, he brake it, and said, Take, eat: this is my body, which is broken for you: this do in remembrance of me. After the same manner also he took the cup, when he had supped, saying, This cup is the new testament in my blood: this do ye, as oft as ye drink it, in remembrance of me. For as often as ye eat this bread, and drink this cup, ye do shew the Lord's death till he come."[18]

It is this supper which gives permanent and clear meaning to His other words, "As Moses lifted up the serpent in the wilderness, even so must the Son of man be lifted up . . . And I, if I be lifted up from the earth, will draw all men unto me."[19]

Surely this is the source from which the early Church drew its very life. "Jesus can save you from your sins!" That is the message men carried across the world. "The blood of Jesus Christ cleanses us from all sin!" That was the Good News. "God was in Christ, reconciling the world unto himself."[20] That was the chief doctrine.

The disciples told the story simply and sincerely: "We are saved by the Christ who died for us, and the symbol of that fact is the Cross." Jesus in His death has saved the world from death.

"I am the way, the truth, and the life," Jesus had said: "no man cometh unto the Father, but by me."[21] "I am the resurrection, and the life: he that believeth in me, though he were dead, yet shall he live: and whosoever liveth and believeth in me shall never die."[22]

It was from the Cross that the Christian Church learned the truth that "sacrifice is the supreme condition of peace and increase of life, that self-surrender is the secret of self-realization."

GOD BELIEVES

"I believe in the Cross because God believes in it. God sent His only begotten Son into the world for the sole purpose of dying! In the "determinate counsel and foreknowledge of God"[23] it was all foreseen. Jesus of Nazareth was the eternal Son in temporal flesh. He was Immanuel, God with us. He was Jesus, the One who should "save his people from their sins."[24] He was the "Lamb of God, which taketh away the sin of the world."[25]

There are many, many theories as to how the Cross saves us from our sins. Our Church accepts one theory and other Churches have their theories. The important thing to remember is that we are not saved by our adherence to any one theory. We are saved by the fact of Christ's death on the cross. *If you accept His death as your basis of life you are right even though your theory of His dying is wrong.*

Put in simple form, the crucifixion means this: God does not hate us. God loves us. He wants to help us. He wants us to have life, abundant and eternal. He does not want us to die and never live. He does not want us to die in sin and thus be sinners forever. He wants man to be on His side, and He paid an infinite price for our salvation.

I have often thought of it. The forensic theory held by most Churches does violence to the nature of God as set forth by Christ. It smacks too much of criminals and courts.

The "Father" Jesus knew was not a "judge" entangled in the phraseology of laws and precedents. He was pure love and pure wisdom! He needed no legal means of pardoning men save their willingness to love and trust Him. This does not mean that we are saved by His life alone! It does not mean that the Cross is unimportant. The Cross is all-important. It is God's final act of saving grace, and is the evidence of grace, God's love toward the unworthy.

In the Cross it is as if God were saying, "I expected too much of man in the garden and on the trail. Now I will make everything right. I myself will bend to befriend him, and if he will, I will lift him into Paradise. I will remove the flashing swords from before Eden and let him come home. I have taught him to lay his hand upon the sacrifice and be identified with it. Now I shall place my hand upon him and be one with him."

Out of the love of God came Jesus to walk the earth and die. In His life He has shown us how we ought to live, and in His death He has removed the seeds of death from us by removing our sins. He rose from the dead to assure us of His living presence and our eternal hope.

The person who died on the cross was not a good man raised Godward. He was God lowered earthward. Nor was He an innocent person compelled to bear our sins in His own body on the tree. He was God of very God who for His own secret reasons declared that the only way whereby we can gain forgiveness and eternal life is by faith in Him and faithfulness in living His kind of life.

C. S. Lewis has said that "A car is made to run on petrol, and it won't run properly on anything else. Now God designed the human machine to run on Himself. He Himself is the fuel."[26]

How could God get Himself into men and women and little children in the earth? God chose the way of the Cross and the Gospel. The plan of salvation is not man-made. It is God-made. The message of the Cross, then, is this: "Christ has put you right with God. God has done everything necessary for your salvation and eternal happiness. But there is something you must do. You must recognize that Jesus died for you, and that He, and He alone, can introduce you to God and get you into heaven."

God does not demand that you understand the mystery that is resident in the Cross. He does not demand that you accept any one of the theories of why Jesus died or how His death saves us. But you must believe that His death is of universal and eternal importance; that it somehow crushes sin and creates new life. You must believe that He died for you.

As our hymn says,

> "There was no other good enough
> To pay the price of sin;
> He only could unlock the gate of heaven,
> And let us in."[27]

Or as the poet sings,

> "I know not how that Calvary's cross
> A world from sin could free;
> I only know its matchless love
> Has brought God's love to me."[28]

I like the words of Abelard who wrote in the twelfth century:

"The purpose and cause of the Incarnation was that He might illuminate the world by His wisdom and excite it to the love of Himself. . . . Our redemption is that supreme love of Christ shown to us by His passion, which not only frees us from slavery to sin, but acquires for us the true liberty of sons of God, so that we fulfill all things, not so much from fear as from love of Him who exhibited so great favor toward us."

Before Christ's Cross, His love in its zenith, I am humble and reverent. He draws me as surely as the moon draws the seas. He makes me tender with His tenderness, forgiving with His kindness, and strong with His purity. When I stand before Him I know the prison doors of self are open and I am free to ascend.

IT IS THE ONLY WAY

I believe in the Cross because it is the only way we can save the world. The individual Christian is supposed to be a person who has accepted Christ's death as the divine mystery whereby man is brought into the presence of God the Father, and whereby he is made sinless and eternal. The individual Christian must grow into a fully surrendered, fully dedicated follower of Christ whose primary task in life is the persuading of mankind that God knew what He was doing and is doing, and that the Christ way is the highway of both holiness and happiness.

The Church, the society made up of these Cross-conscious individuals, is supposed to be a Cross-conscious congregation. It is the community of the dedicated, the fully surrendered. It is the congregation of those who are striving to be worthy of God's love and blessing. Thence the Church is the society of the redeemed. As the redeemed the Church must itself become the redeemer. Its task is more than the perpetuation of the words of Jesus. It must make concrete the purpose of Jesus, the redemption of the world from sin. We were once raw ore in the hills of life. We have been mined and smelted and molded and we are now supposed to be instruments of salvation in the hands of God.

As the society of the redeemed we are supposed to be good people. But we are supposed to be more than good people. We are supposed to be God's people. We are His body. We are Christ, the physical part of Christ. We have given Him our lives. We have emptied our bodies of self that He may dwell in us. Think of it! We are His body. Therefore we are Christ. *We supply the body and He supplies the life within that body.* Even as He gave His body in the work of redemption, so must the Church. Hence the body of Christ, the society of believers, must empty itself of its frail humanity in order to be filled with strong divinity.

Even as God was in Christ reconciling the world unto Himself, so must God be in the Church reconciling the world unto Himself. *The Christian Church is the continuing Christ on earth.*

But if we permit the body to be weak and old, devoid of strength and vision, can Christ speak through us to a sinful, needy world?

The product of the Church, the member of the Church, should be an intelligent person who has accepted Christ as God's eternal Son, who lived and was crucified for our salvation, and who lives forever as the source of our daily power. The product of the Church must be a Christian in whose life the moral, ethical, and spiritual laws of Christ are radiantly made manifest. *The Christian Church must produce Christlike people or forfeit its claim to be the body of our Lord.*

He came to teach, to heal, to comfort, and to challenge. He came to condemn and reconstruct, amend and complete, enlighten and enliven. He came to align a bent world to the wishes of God. So full was His love, so large His self-forgetfulness, that the Cross is but the closing chapter in the greatest love story ever told.

If the Church, His body, is to express His love, it must be willing to do all He did, even unto death.

Sin, man's unwillingness to let God live within him; sin, man's refusal to be Christ's body, lies at the bottom of all the ills of our world. Things will not be better until the Christ of the Cross becomes the Christ of our hearts; until the Cross itself becomes our platform of worship and service.

Too long have we been saying, "I believe in the crucifixion, but . . .!" Today is the day when we must cry with the saints of the ages, "I am determined not to know anything . . . save Jesus Christ, and him crucified . . . for I am crucified with Christ."[29]

CHAPTER EIGHT

"I Believe in the Ascendant Christ, But ..."

(ACTS 7:54-60)

ತ•

WHEN PETER ARRIVED at the house of Cornelius he spoke these very impressive words, words that disclose, not merely the faith of the early Church, but the source of that faith:

"Of a truth I perceive that God is no respecter of persons: but in every nation he that feareth him, and worketh righteousness, is accepted with him. The word which God sent unto the children of Israel, preaching peace by Jesus Christ: (he is Lord of all:) that word, I say, ye know, which was published throughout all Judaea, and began from Galilee, after the baptism which John preached; how God anointed Jesus of Nazareth with the Holy Ghost and with power: who went about doing good, and healing all that were oppressed of the devil; for God was with him. And we are witnesses of all things which he did both in the land of the Jews, and in Jerusalem; whom they slew and hanged on a tree: him God raised up the third day, and shewed him openly; not to all the people, but unto witnesses chosen before of God, even to us, who did eat and drink with him after he rose from the dead. And he commanded us to preach unto the people, and to testify that it is he which was ordained of God to be the Judge of quick and dead. To him give all the prophets witness, that through his name whosoever believeth in him shall receive remission of sins."[1]

Here then is the Apostles' Creed in narrative form, "Was crucified, dead, and buried; He descended into Hades; the third day He rose again from the dead." And Peter might have added here what he believed and what, in substance, he added elsewhere, "He ascended into heaven; and sitteth on the right hand of God the Father Almighty; from thence He shall come to judge the quick and the dead."[2]

The words in this passage to which I call your special attention are these, "And he commanded us to preach unto the people, and to testify that it is he which was ordained of God to be the Judge of quick [living] and dead." In other words, during the post-Resurrection period, the forty days when Jesus appeared and disappeared, it seems clear that He instructed the apostles concerning what they should believe and what they should preach. They were not left to decide for themselves what they should say concerning Christ's life and death, His resurrection and ascension. Jesus instructed them from the Old Testament, and from His own ministry, concerning what they should believe and teach. They were thus fully prepared to share with the world the full mystery of the person and promises of Christ.

We sometimes wonder why the apostles were so convinced of Christ's pre-existence, His deity, His unique relationship with God, the full meaning of the atonement, the resurrection, and life to be. May we not say, and say with sufficient support of Scripture to make it more valid than a guess and a wish, that Jesus shared with them during the forty days many unknown portions of His earthly life — for example, the temptation in the wilderness, the story of His birth as He remembered it from the lips of Mary — and may we not also believe that He explained God's purposes and promises so completely that, as far as they could absorb them, His teachings adequately prepared them for a vital, truth-filled ministry?

This message needs but one main point, one solid affirmation, *I believe in the Ascendant Christ because the apostles believed in Him.* The cry of the Apostle Paul is added to the voice of Peter, and becomes the larger anthem of thanksgiving and praise, "Now is Christ risen from the dead, and become the firstfruits of them that slept. . . . Death is swallowed up in victory. O death, where is thy sting? O grave, where is thy victory? . . . But thanks be to God, which giveth us the victory through our Lord Jesus Christ."[3] "For to me to live is Christ, and to die is gain."[4] "Who shall separate us from the love of Christ? shall tribulation, or distress, or persecution, or famine, or nakedness, or peril, or sword? . . . Nay, in all these things we are more than conquerors through him that loved us. For I am persuaded, that neither death, nor life, nor angels, nor principalities, nor powers, nor things present, nor things to come, nor height, nor depth, nor any other creature, shall be able to separate us from the love of God, which is in Christ Jesus our Lord."[5] "I would not have you to be ignorant, brethren, concerning them which are asleep, that ye sorrow not, even as others which have no hope. For if we believe that Jesus died and rose again, even so them also which sleep in Jesus will God bring with him."[6]

That is the voice of the early Christians. That is the good news written into every page of the New Testament. It was the very core of the Church's convictions. It was the golden foundation of courage, faith, and hope. It was the good news of God, that men through faith in Jesus Christ should live forever. Death would rob them of their bodies. Death would separate them in physical form from loved ones who continued in physical form, but death could not rob them of personal identity, and death could not condemn them to the ghostly sphere of a misty hereafter. Death for them was but the threshold to the Father's House, the doorway to eternal joy and love.

Many have asked me the question: What was it that made the early Church such a power? What was it that made the apostles and early Christians fearless of life and death and faithful to God? I say to you that it was the doctrine of the risen, ascendant Christ, coupled with the firm conviction that at the moment of death Christians were lifted into the very presence of Christ and rewarded for their faithfulness. It was this faith that moved Christians to walk the earth with the grace and fearlessness of kingly lions. It was this faith that moved them to sing songs of praise in the presence of death, to face courageously the edicts of kings and princes, and to preach the Word of God in its stark purity.

No wonder Paul concluded his great resurrection chapter with the word, "Therefore, my beloved brethren, be ye stedfast, unmovable, always abounding in the work of the Lord, forasmuch as ye know that your labour is not in vain in the Lord."[7] Why? Because Christ was alive! He was not dead! And they were alive in Him, and would be alive forevermore. God is the God of the living and the living dead! Alleluia!

Put yourself in the shoes of any of the apostles. Suppose you had walked the earth for three years with the noblest personality that ever brought silver dawn into the hearts of men. Suppose you had listened to His words, watched His every act, and knew Him as intimately as a mother knows her child. Would not your story run like this: "Yes, I heard Him speak of life to be. But you see, we already knew that the dead die not. Every Jew knew that, except, of course, the

Sadducees. Every Jew knew that when you die you descend into Sheol, the land of the departed spirits, where you wander until the day of resurrection. No Jew delighted in the prospect. The lowest beggar on earth was better off than a king in Sheol. We knew all that, but we did not know what He meant when He talked about rising from the grave in three days. He prophesied the event. He tried to prepare us, but how could we be readied? To us the resurrection meant only one thing: at the end of time the dead would be called before God and judged. We did not understand. Then He died! We saw Him there on the cross. We saw the Roman guard drive the spear into His side. We saw the limp body lifted down and buried in the sepulchre. We saw the stone rolled into place. With tears streaming down our faces we departed. I remember putting my arm around Peter and sobbing, 'It is all over, Peter. He is gone forever. We will never see Him again. The golden dream is made of clay after all.' Then we went into hiding. It seems cowardly now, but remember, if the leaders were out to break up the new religious movement they would want us as well as Christ. That is why we hid. There in hiding we cried and talked, each recalling some brilliant moment in the life of Him who was not only born under a new bright star, but was a bright new star in the knowledge and appreciation of men. The dawn that had seemed so beautiful and wonderful grew into the dimness of evening, and hope crawled into a dark corner and shivered with apprehension.

"That is what we did, and that is exactly what you would have done. And when Easter morning came with its startling news of the empty tomb we incredulously went to see for ourselves. We looked at the empty graveclothes and shook our heads in stupid misery. We questioned the gardener and all others who were in the neighborhood. We searched in the bushes and field, thinking that some prankster had carried away the body. We looked at the women, and especially at Mary, and said, 'It is too bad! Grief has robbed them all of their reason.' And the events of Easter morning made us even more miserable.

"Had you been there you would have been like Thomas who said, 'Except I shall see in his hands the print of the nails, and put my finger into the print of the nails, and thrust my hand into his side, I will not believe.'[8]

"Then in the evening, we sat down to our sunset meal; our hearts and minds already clouded by the black night of grief. We were completely defeated by sorrow, and then we heard a voice, 'Peace be unto you,' and there He was! He, the One whom we saw die, the One they laid in the grave! It was He! It was the same body, the same Jesus. The same, and yet not the same. It had strange powers. It seemed enveloped in a mist of otherness, so that you had to look closely to localize and apprehend it.

"Had you been there, you would have slept fitfully that night, and with the dawn would have come the question, 'Did we really see Him?' Was it a dream, an hallucination born of grief? You would have thought so, even as we did. But He came again, and again, and again; not just to us, but unto larger groups, and unto other individuals. We heard His words of instruction. We grew used to His going and coming, appearing and disappearing. By the end of the forty days we were convinced that He was He, the One whom we had known intimately, and who died and was buried.

"Henceforth the empty tomb was the symbol of our own full hearts. There was no questioning now. We were filled with a thrilling joy. We were rich in confidence. We had a message for the world. We had good news for all! This experience had transformed our fears into vibrant faith. This period of instruction had placed in our hands the golden keys of heaven. We were now citizens of two worlds. We lived here, but we were convinced by actuality that death would mean merely entering another room in the House of God.

"Each Sunday He came back. We grew used to His coming on the first day of the week, and that first day became so important, so informative and inspiring, that we, good Jews that we were, soon created a long week end, a week with two Sabbaths, the Sabbath of the Law and the Sabbath of Christ's love. Jesus even suggested that we drop the old Sabbath, pointing out that the law of Moses had now given place to the law of the Christ, and henceforth believers were to begin the week with worship. Thus the Lord's Day was born, and while many of us continued to keep the ancient Sabbath from force of habit and association, it was the Lord's Day that became our time of praise and joy!

"And then one day He disappeared and did not come back. It troubled us at first, but then the Holy Spirit came, and we felt Christ's nearness in the Spirit's blessing. Whenever we spoke in behalf of Christ, whenever we stretched forth our hands to help another, whenever we shared the wonders of His life and love and resurrection, we felt an inner warmth, a conviction of faith, we knew He was near! We felt He was walking the earth with us, helping us as we would let Him help, building us up in faith and courage, and brightening our understanding. We knew Him, not as a ghost in some vague beyond, but as an actual person, living and real, and vitally interested in the spreading of the Gospel. He was not the dead Christ to us, nor the ghost-Christ, nor the absent Christ. He was the ascendant Christ, the one we had seen after the resurrection, the one who had talked with us and instructed us, the one who sent us forth to preach the Word and to live in kindness."

That is the experience the apostles had. That is what transformed them from men filled with fear to men filled with faith. That is what sent them forth to preach and die for Him. They knew they were eternal beings who at the moment of death would go immediately to be with the Ascendant Jesus!

For more than a hundred years that was exactly the feeling of the Christian Church. Death to the early Christians was graduation day, their true commencement. They did not sing it, but they certainly lived the hymn, "I'm Bound for the Promised Land."

Stephen, kneeling in the street wherein the footsteps of death were growing louder, looked up and knew that the Lord was just above his head, and gave utterance to the conviction of the early Church, "Lord Jesus, receive my spirit."[9] There was no question in his mind as to what lay before him. The Ascendant Jesus was there — waiting! In a few moments more he and Jesus would be together forever.

Faith then was like a marching army, with banners in the wind, with trumpets burnished and blaring, with men advancing steadily, rank on rank. Christians then did not talk down the high thoughts of the Christ, watering strong truth in behalf of weak Christians. They did not cross their fingers every time they mentioned the atonement, the resurrection, and the ascension. They did not live as if shackled by question marks concerning what lay beyond the grave.

There are some things in Christianity that must ride the heavens like the sun and stars. True, they are too high for our grasp, but their height should not move us to question their reality. The deity of Jesus is one, the atonement and the resurrection are others, and the living, ascendant, victorious Christ must be supreme above them all.

Here let me say a word about the "descending Christ." It is regrettable that our Creed reads, "He descended into *hell*." Hell is the land of the unredeemable dead. That hell is a part of Scriptural teachings all must admit. It represents final separation from God and all that is good, and whether it be cold or hot it represents the dead-end street of the lost.

The word itself is not an old word. It is a Saxon word meaning "a hole," "a grave," "a hiding place." But in its theological usage it is more than these. It is the final depository of all that is not of God. It is the place of refuse from which nothing can be salvaged. I personally resent the statement that Jesus visited such a place. If none can be salvaged from hell why should He go there at all?

Yet both Peter and Paul seem to suggest that He did visit Hades, the land of the living dead, and that something wonderful did happen during the days Jesus was in the grave.[10] Our Creed says of Christ, "crucified, dead, and buried." But the Creed does not end there. The early Church believed there was more to it than that.[11] It was for this reason that the Church added the words, "He descended into Hades."

Now Hades is not the same as hell. Hell is the resting place of those who are lost forever. Hades is the resting place of the living dead, some heaven-bound and some hell-bound. Hell, looking at it from a human geographical standpoint, must be on the other side of Hades, even as I believe heaven is. After the final Judgment many who are in Hades will enter the final heaven, and others will be condemned to follow their chosen ways in regions which are not heavenly.

Here let me also make a difference between Paradise and

heaven. Even as I believe that hell is a place beyond Hades so I believe that heaven is. Between here and hell there is a part of Hades which contains those who shall eventually be condemned. Between here and heaven there is a part of Hades which contains those who shall eventually enter heaven. And is it not just possible, and I realize that this is pure speculation, but is it not just possible that Hades also contains those whose final destiny is not settled during life on earth for the simple reason that they had no adequate opportunity of accepting or rejecting Jesus Christ as Redeemer?

Following this speculative path, is it not just possible that during the time Jesus was in the grave He visited Hades and there spoke to the dead whose final destiny was not fixed at death? Is this what Peter and Paul had in mind? Is not this exactly what the early Church believed?[12]

As I have studied the subject I see no reason why we should not call that part of Hades which contains the heaven-bound dead, Paradise. At death we go to Paradise, and for us this will be heaven until the Judgment is past and the "new heaven" becomes our home. May not this Paradise be the place Scripture has in mind when it speaks of Jesus' being at the "right hand of God"?[13]

To say, as our Church says, that "The souls of believers are at their death made perfect in holiness,"[14] does not rule out the Paradise existence. Nor does it prohibit our believing in a period of development during our Paradise days which precede the heaven days, not in a purgatorial manner, but in a garden manner. Our God believes in slow growth toward perfection. And when our Church says that at death believers immediately pass into glory, it need not push the idea of "glory" beyond the Paradise existence which prepares us for heaven.

I would not press the idea of an intermediary state too far, but I do not believe it should be ignored. It has been part of the thinking of the Christian Church from the days of the apostles. Our knowledge of that "other life" is meager. I sometimes feel that some of our doctrines suffer from inflation. We claim too much. I believe we should grasp all views of all subjects and strive to squeeze from them whatever juices they contain for the healing of our hearts and the drying of our tears. I realize that the idea of an intermediary state is a controversial subject, and that many in the Church would not agree with me, nor am I courting argument, but I do desire to turn an open mind toward this great area of our hopes.

Let me then present my thought in a different way: I believe that as a believer I am growing toward Christlikeness: personal completion in God. Part of the process takes place here and part hereafter. All the distance I cover here is gain there. Hence, it makes no great difference when I die so long as I am living toward Him and the completion He has commanded me to attain. Such a view makes sense to me as does its accompanying one, namely, that I believe that God will give every human being, either here or hereafter, an adequate opportunity to accept or reject Jesus Christ as Lord and Redeemer.

The idea of purgatorial fires wherein believers are purified is abhorrent to me, as is the teaching that men may ignore Christ here and have another opportunity to accept or reject Him after death. Both purgatory and second probation are unscriptural, and not even speculation can give them a garment of respectability.

Jesus said, "In my Father's house are many home-places." I believe it, and I believe that in them all, the home-places here, the home-places in Paradise, and the home-places in the final heaven, believers have the privilege of walking with Him and growing into His likeness. The eternal pilgrimage is a challenge and a comfort to my heart.

There is no time here to speak of either heaven or hell and their meaning. That must come later, but I do want to share with you this bit of verse that has meant much to me:

"Think of ....
Stepping on shore, and finding it Heaven!
Of taking hold of a hand, and finding it God's hand;
Of breathing a new air, and finding it celestial air;
Of feeling invigorated, and finding it immortality;
Of passing from storm and tempest to an unbroken calm;
Of waking up, and finding it home."[15]

Dr. Paterson-Smyth, in *The Gospel of the Hereafter*, says:

"The Lord is risen, but the people do not know it. There is no death, but the people do not believe it. . . . What is the matter with us, Christian people? Do we not know? Or have we lost our beliefs? Or has imagination grown dulled by too frequent repetition of God's good news?"[16]

He goes on to point out that while we are now God's caterpillars, we will some day be God's butterflies; while we are now God's acorns, we will some day be God's oaks; while we are now God's dry little seeds, we shall eventually be part of God's golden harvest.

The Apostle John wrote saying, "Now are we the sons of God, and it doth not yet appear what we shall be: but we know that, when he shall appear, we shall be like him; for we shall see him as he is."[17]

Sursum corda, O Christian people! Lift up your hearts. The Lord is risen! The Lord has ascended on high leading captivity captive. There is no death!

CHAPTER NINE

"I Believe in the Judgment, But ... "

(MATTHEW 25:31-46)

ろ✍

PLATO in his *Republic* relates the story of the trance of Erus. Erus was wounded in battle and left to die. Later he revived and told how he had left this world in a never-ceasing flow of souls journeying to the other world. There the stream was divided, the just taking the road to the right, and the unjust the road to the left. The just were thus received into heaven while the unjust were condemned to return to the earth and live again in some hideous animal or insect form. When Erus appeared he was commanded by the eternal judges to return to the earth and tell all men that after death they are to be judged by the lives they live on earth.[1]

Modern man does not want to believe this. Modern man grows irritable when he is asked the question, "Where will you spend eternity?" He says he is not interested in eternity. Earth is heaven and hell enough, and every day is judgment day. Modern man, as O. A. Curtis has observed, "is a heathen mystic made superficially hopeful by a Christian atmosphere."[2]

Tertullian, the great Christian theologian of North Africa, once said to his people, "You are fond of spectacles except the greatest of all spectacles, the last and eternal judgment."

For all Biblical Christians the judgment is as real as taxes. We know that eternity is before us. We also know that life here is to be related to life there. We know that we are morally accountable and that the time shall surely come when we must answer to Him whose name is God.

We are those of whom John Masefield sings,

"Friends and loves we have none, nor wealth nor blest abode,
But the hope of the City of God at the other end of the road.

"Not for us are content, and quiet, and peace of mind,
For we go seeking a city that we shall never find.

"There is no solace on earth for us — for such as we —
Who search for a hidden city that we shall never see.

"Only the road and the dawn, the sun, the wind, and the rain,
And the watch fires under stars, and sleep, and the road again.

"We seek the City of God, and the haunt where beauty dwells,
And we find the noisy mart and the sound of burial bells.

"Never the golden city, where radiant people meet,
But the dolorous town where mourners are going about the street.

"We travel the dusty road 'till the light of the day is dim,
And sunset shows us spires away on the world's rim.

"We travel from dawn to dusk, till the day is past and by,
Seeking the Holy City beyond the rim of the sky.

"Friends and loves we have none, nor wealth nor blest abode,
But the hope of the City of God at the other end of the road."[3]

Not only do we seek the City of God at the other end of the road, but we know that we must pause at the City's gate and wait until the books are opened and we have been judged.

I believe in the judgment because humanity as a whole believes in it. It is strange that while different races have different ideas of God and morality, sin and righteousness, heaven and hell, all believe in an almighty being called God; all believe in sin; all feel that they have broken the divine law and must placate God; all believe in sacrificial offerings; all believe that by doing certain things they can win God's favor, His blessing and forgiveness; all believe that on the other side of death men will be rewarded or punished according to the lives they have lived here, and all believe in a place of reward and a place of punishment beyond death.

The Hebrew with his Sheol, the Greek with his Hades, join with the numerous other peoples in registering their conviction that we not only live beyond the grave but that we shall be judged beyond the grave for the lives we have lived on earth.

All men everywhere and at all times have felt that this judgment is necessary for the equalizing of life, for the balancing of the inequities men endure on earth.

Job knew, and man has always known, that we get neither our full blessings nor our full punishments here on earth. Over and over again the sinful prosper and are gay while the righteous suffer and are sad. Too often the sinner inherits the earth while the saint begs at the gate of Dives. In every language the problem of Job and of Lazarus is told. Life is not balanced in such a manner that the good get what they deserve and the evil get what they deserve. Therefore all languages carry the story of man's conviction that sometime, somewhere, things will be different and justice will be done.

In all nations and in all generations you will find those whom we would classify as naturalistic or materialistic. They do not believe in life to be. They laugh and scorn the hopes and fears of 99 percent of the human family. When you die, they say, you are dead forever. You are chemistry, not spirit. You are body, not soul. You live once and there is no judgment save that of the laws of life and the grave.

You will also find those who feel that God will make everything all right regardless of how we live on earth. We speak of these people as the Universalists. They build their hopes on the benevolence of God, His unwillingness that any of His children should be lost.

Speaking of the so-called Christian Universalists I feel they are false to the clear teachings of Scripture and to our own inner convictions. The record of mankind does not substantiate their claims, and neither does a clear-eyed study of the Bible. Certainly Jesus did not teach any such theory.

I presume that a third group could also be found, those who believe that regardless of how they live life now they will get a second chance beyond the grave. In Christian theology these are those who believe in second probation, a second chance. Over there, they argue, God will so arrange matters that they can no longer refuse to love and serve Him, and so they feel there is no reason why they should get excited over religion now.

Scripture gives us no evidence of such a probation. Christian teaching on this point is summed up by the writer of the book of Hebrews when he says, "It is appointed unto men once to die, but after this the judgment."[4] The universalist theory is bad economics. If God could save us over there it was foolish of Him to try to save us here.

No, as one studies the beliefs of the races and nations that have inhabited this planet he finds that as men enter eternity they are divided, some on the left and the others on the right. Mankind rises to declare this day: There is to be a judgment!

I believe in the judgment because it is the clear teaching of the Bible. The First Psalm says that "the ungodly shall not stand [in his own defense] in the judgment."[5] On that day there will be no need of words from him. The record will be complete.

The writer of the book of Ecclesiastes ends his interesting dissertation with these words, "Let us hear the conclusion of the whole matter: Fear God, and keep his commandments: for this is the whole duty of man. For God shall bring every work into judgment, with every secret thing, whether it be good, or whether it be evil."[6]

This is the teaching of the Old Testament. As Isaiah has expressed it, God will "not judge after the sight of his eyes, neither reprove after the hearing of his ears: but with right-eousness shall he judge the poor, and reprove with equity for the meek of the earth: and he shall smite the earth with the rod of his mouth, and with the breath of his lips shall he slay the wicked."[7]

When you come to the New Testament it is even more clear. Jesus was very conscious of having left God in order to come into the world, and equally convinced of returning to His former position with God after He had completed His mission here. He was also conscious of judgment. In the fifth chapter of John we read, "For as the Father raiseth up the dead, and quickeneth them [maketh them alive]; even so the Son quickeneth whom he will. For the Father judgeth no man, but hath committed all judgment unto the Son: that all men should honour the Son, even as they honour the Father. He that honoureth not the Son honoureth not the Father which hath sent him. Verily, verily, I say unto you, He that heareth my word, and believeth on him that sent me, hath everlasting life, and shall not come into condemnation; but is passed from death unto life. . . . For as the Father hath life in himself; so hath he given to the Son to have life in him-self; and hath given him authority to execute judgment also . . . Marvel not at this: for the hour is coming, in the which all that are in the graves shall hear his voice, and shall come forth; they that have done good, unto the resurrection of life; and they that have done evil, unto the resurrection of damnation."[8]

Paul in the fourteenth chapter of Romans affirms that, "we shall all stand before the judgment seat of Christ."[9] In the fifth chapter of Second Corinthians he says, "For we must all appear before the judgment seat of Christ; that every one may receive the things done in his body, according to that he hath done, whether it be good or bad."[10] In his letter to Timothy we hear Paul declaring, "I have fought a good fight, I have finished my course, I have kept the faith: henceforth there is laid up for me a crown of righteousness, which the Lord, the righteous judge, shall give me at that day: and not to me only, but unto all them also that love his appearing."[11]

And what shall we say to these words of Jesus? "When the Son of man shall come in his glory, and all the holy angels with him, then shall he sit upon the throne of his glory: and before him shall be gathered all nations: and he shall separate them one from another, as a shepherd divideth his sheep from the goats: and he shall set the sheep on his right hand, but the goats on the left. Then shall the King say unto them on his right hand, Come, ye blessed of my Father, inherit the kingdom prepared for you from the foundation of the world: for I was an hungred, and ye gave me meat: I was thirsty, and ye gave me drink: I was a stranger, and ye took me in: naked, and ye clothed me: I was sick, and ye visited me: I was in prison, and ye came unto me. Then shall the righteous answer him, saying, Lord, when saw we thee an hungred, and fed thee? or thirsty, and gave thee drink? When saw we thee a stranger, and took thee in? or naked, and clothed thee? Or when saw we thee sick, or in prison, and came unto thee? And the King shall answer and say unto them, Verily I say unto you, Inasmuch as ye have done it unto one of the least of these my brethren, ye have done it unto me. Then shall he say also unto them on the left hand, Depart from me, ye cursed, into everlasting fire, prepared for the devil and his angels: for I was an hungred, and ye gave me no meat:I was thirsty, and ye gave me no drink: I was a stranger, and ye took me not in: naked, and ye clothed me not: sick, and in prison, and ye visited me not. Then shall they also answer him, saying, Lord, when saw we thee an hungred, or athirst, or a stranger, or naked, or sick, or in prison, and did not minister unto thee? Then shall he answer them, saying, Verily I say unto you, Inasmuch as ye did it not to one of the least of these, ye did it not to me. And these shall go away into everlasting punishment: but the righteous into life eternal."[12]

Here we may pause before the awesome question of Peter, "If the righteous [the Christians] scarcely be saved, where shall the ungodly and the sinner appear?"[13]

I believe in the judgment because it is the conviction of the historic Church. Our oldest creed therefore rightly says, "From thence He shall come to judge the quick and the dead."

Christianity has always set its sights on eternity. Not on earth shall we know the full and joyful story of salvation. Not here, amidst the rubble of sin's destruction, shall we see Christ in all the wonder of His love. Not here shall the good be rewarded and the evil crushed. Here the wheat and the false wheat must grow together until the harvest. Here the good and the bad fish swim together in the sea called life. But there shall be a day when humanity shall be divided, left and right, and God, the righteous Judge, will bless and ban.

It has always been the teaching of the Church that earth is not our home nor our destiny. We are headed for something beyond. Jesus was very conscious of this fact, and so was Paul.

Paul said that to die was to be "at home with the Lord."[14] Jesus said, "I go to prepare a place for you."[15]

Nothing is clearer in Holy Writ than the fact that Jesus was convinced that only in that other world, that next life, shall we understand the meaning of existence and the meaning of God.

Christians used to sing, "I Am Bound for the Promised Land," "There's a Land That Is Fairer Than Day," "The City Four-Square," and other hymns of heaven. And we should! Our destiny is not on earth! Salvation has no large and regal significance if it does not concern the life to be. To be saved from sin is meaningless if it saves us not from death, for death, as Paul taught, is the fruit of sin. If sins are slain, then death is defeated.

We have often said, "The blood of the martyrs is the seed of the Church." I wish we could believe that the confidence of the martyrs should be ours. They counted it a privilege to die for Christ. They sang and said with Justin Martyr, "This is my victory day. Today I shall see God."

Not only does historic Christianity believe in life beyond death, thus adding its voice to all the religions of the ages, but Christianity believes that over there we shall be judged by what we are here. I stress *what we are,* or better yet, *what we are trying to be,* rather than what we believe, for I am more and more persuaded that a man may be right in his heart and wrong in his head, and that in all probability God is going to judge us by our quality of life rather than by our opinions. He knows what we want to be and do. He knows how hard we fight for mastery over bad habits. He will credit us for accepting and trying to live Christian lives.

There shall be a day of final reckoning. That is the teaching of Christianity. The time shall come when the books will be opened and we shall be called to account for the deeds done in the body. Two sets of books shall be opened, say the Scriptures, and whatever the first books say will be judged by the presence of our names in God's Book of Life.

It is our teaching that because eternity is before us, and because God wanted us to face it with confidence and hope, Jesus came. God knew that there is in humanity a drift toward darkness, a drift toward death. He also knew that something must be done to create a drift toward light and life. He knew, as we never know, that a man to live a full moral life must be in constant companionship with God, and that only as man moves closer and closer to God, and therefore closer and closer to light and life, can eternity be more than a dark dread.

In all our mouthings about original sin, may we not add this clarifying thought: There is in every man the seeds of darkness and death. There is in every man the seeds of spiritual doom. The harvest of such seeds can only be prevented by a supreme act of love on the part of God, and therefore God sent Christ to show man the light and to lead Him toward the source of life. Christ is the Gardener who destroys the seeds of darkness and death, and maketh the good to grow. Thus Paul could say that by one man's disobedience death had come into the world, and by one man's obedience, death was swallowed up in victory.

Man is spiritually dead until God becomes a living reality in him. Man is without living hope until he realizes that the drift toward darkness and death can be halted and reversed only by the leadership of Christ. To die physically is not a matter of little consequence save to those who are truly God's. We all must die physically. We need not all die spiritually. Spiritual death added to physical death means separation from God forever and forever.

All of us must die. That fact is as real as March 15! But dying physically is the lesser of two possible deaths. To die spiritually is to die with finality. It is my conviction, therefore, that whatever path we walk in this life shall determine the direction we walk in the life to be. If in this life we walk toward God, surely in the next world we shall come to Him. If, however, in this life we walk away from Him, shall not the path in the hereafter lead us onward and downward to a place where God is not? There is to be a heaven, and there is to be a hell. It makes no difference to me whether hell is 12,000 degrees Fahrenheit or 168 below zero. Temperature has nothing to do with it. That is but a symbol. If in that other life we come to a place where God and goodness are absent, where beauty never smiles and where kindness never sings, believe me, that will be hell.

Jesus is important because He is the Way, the Truth, and the Life. He is in the light, and we who believe are in the light. In the light we love. In the light we do not stumble. In the light we fear not the darkness, nay, not even the darkness of death.

No wonder the Apostle could cry with jubilation, "So when this corruptible shall have put on incorruption, and this mortal shall have put on immortality, then shall be brought to pass the saying that is written, Death is swallowed up in victory."[16]

Personally, I believe in an intermediate state between here and both heaven and hell. For some it will be purgatorial fire, but not the fire that cleanses. For others it will be the very presence of the Christ and the peace that passeth understanding. There, as John Wesley once said, "the saints will be continually ripening for harvest." There we shall know Christ as we are known. There we shall know love in its fullest loveliness, and sin in all its human ugliness. There our education will go on and we will know the mind of God and the heart of God and be filled with new knowledge and new love.

At the end of time when this little earth shall have served its purpose, humanity as we know it will come to an end and God will establish the new heaven and the new earth. Then shall be the judgment, and all those who are found worthy shall be called to the right hand of the Father and shall become the citizens of God's new world.

One wonderful fact is apparent here: Jesus Christ shall be the Judge.[17] He who shared our humanity, who walked our roads and streets, who talked with men of every trade in all places of our busy life, shall Himself be Judge. For all of us who have owned Him Lord, and have knelt in appreciation and devotion before the place of His cross and His burial, it shall be a time when we behold His smile and not His frown, and we shall enter into heaven. But let this truth be written large upon your hearts: Not even Jesus Christ can help you if you turn your back on Him and refuse to surrender your life into His hands. That is what He meant when He said, "He that believeth on him is not condemned: but he that believeth not is condemned already, because he hath not believed in the name of the only begotten Son of God."[18] To this the writer of Hebrews adds this warning, "How shall we escape, if we neglect so great salvation . . . ?"[19]

In 1867 a young nobleman from France called upon Dr. Forbes Winslow of England, saying that he could not sleep and needed help. Dr. Winslow asked him, "Have you lost money?" "No." "Have you suffered in honor and reputation?" "No." "Have you lost loved ones?" "Not recently." "Then what are you concerned about?" To this last question the young Frenchman replied, "Sir, I am an infidel. My father was an infidel. I have become convinced that there will be life after death and I cannot sleep for thinking about it. If there is to be life beyond the grave, what is to happen to me? Dr. Winslow, can you tell me where I will spend eternity?"

Dr. Winslow replied, "No, I cannot tell you where you will spend eternity, but I know someone who can." He then quoted Isaiah 53:5, "He was wounded for our transgressions, he was bruised for our iniquities: the chastisement of our peace was upon him; and with his stripes we are healed." "That One," said Dr. Winslow, "is the only doctor in the world who can help you." "But," objected the young man, "surely you do not believe all that nonsense, you the leading mind doctor in England, a man of education and science; surely you do not believe that greatest of all Christian superstitions." "But I do believe," replied Dr. Winslow, "I believe in Jesus Christ as my Lord and Saviour. If I did not, I would be like you."

I would like to come to death as Dr. D. L. Moody did. As the life sands slipped from the hourglass he said to his loved ones and friends, "This is my coronation day! I have long been looking forward to it."

Where will you spend eternity? If you wait until then to find out it will be too late. But you can decide the matter now, this day! "For God so loved the world, that he gave his only begotten Son, that whosoever believeth in him should not perish, but have everlasting life."[20]

Do not live as if you were saying, "Yes, I believe in the judgment, but . . ." Rather, live as if you were saying to the world, "Yes, I believe in the judgment, but I fear it not, for I am one with Christ who is my Saviour and Friend forever and forever."

CHAPTER TEN

"I Believe in the Holy Ghost, But..."

(ACTS 1:1-8; 2:1-4)

ૐ

IF SOME SUPER-DARING clergyman, speaking some Sunday morning from a noted pulpit, should announce to his people that the Holy Ghost was dead, one portion of his congregation would be informed enough to resent the blasphemy, another part would try to recall in which of the radio murder dramas the Holy Ghost was cast, and the third part would whisper to the fourth part, "If these communists keep on there will not be a democratic statesman left in the whole of Europe."

Since most modern Christians make no attempt to understand the doctrines of the Church or to face seriously the great problems of the Bible, especially doctrines like the Trinity, it is not surprising that there is great ignorance abroad concerning the Holy Ghost. Like the twelve men Paul met at Ephesus on his third missionary journey, many in the Christian churches of today can say, "We have not so much as heard whether there be any Holy Ghost."[1]

To many of our people phrases like "In the Name of the Father, and of the Son, and of the Holy Ghost" fall within the category of antiques which are to be kept and cherished merely because they are old. We like to think that the use of such phrases links us to the great past of the Church and should be continued in use to add a sense of age and venerability to modern Christianity. We do not sense, that which our fathers felt deeply, that these words represent great truth and should be cherished and used because they help us understand our faith.

I do not claim to understand the great doctrine of the Holy Trinity. It is still incomprehensible. In spite of the fact that I have read much and thought much concerning its various facets it defeats my powers of comprehension.

How can you have three persons in one God, and how can one God be a person when He is composed of three persons? In such a concept how can each be co-equal and co-extensive? How can each be all-wise, all-powerful, and omnipresent? How can you secure unity in such diversity? How can you believe in one God when you have three Gods?

I have gone over and over the ground trying to find answers. There was a time when I liked the idea of the three being but different poses of the one. Since the word "person" comes from the Latin word *"persona,"* and since *persona* meant a mask which an actor wore in a drama, I argued that when we talked of persons in the Godhead we were merely indicating that the one God appeared to us to act three roles: Father, Son, and Holy Ghost. I liked that until I realized it could not be so. Jesus did not feel that He was at once both Son and Father. When He was here He felt that the Father was somewhere else, and that the Holy Ghost was yet to come. True, He said, "I and my Father are one,"[2] but when you list all His statements concerning the Father and the Holy Spirit the idea of God merely changing masks, merely playing different roles, must be ruled out.

There was a time when I was somewhat charmed by the simplicity of St. Patrick's illustration. When the wild Irish chieftain asked him to explain the Trinity, the great saint plucked from the grass a clover leaf, and said, "Here it is: one leaf, yet three."

It is said that the Irish chief was satisfied, which can only mean that the Irish of that day had none of George Bernard Shaw's argumentative blood in their veins. The Irish have made considerable progress since the days of St. Patrick, and no Irishman of this century would accept the saint's illustration. After all, the clover leaf is not three leaves, and the three portions of the one leaf do not have separate identities, nor is there on record a statement that a segment of a clover leaf separated itself from the others and made a trip to Spain or lived a separate existence even for a brief period of time.

I have also thought of God the Father in terms of the sun. It lies far out in space and is untouchable. God is like that, I have reasoned. He has identity outside our world but has a direct influence on our world. God is like the distant sun. Both are sources of light and life. The Son of God might then be likened unto the solar rays that come to us from the sun. They are in a sense the sun, and yet they are not the sun. Year after year I see these invisible rays become flesh and dwell in our midst. What is an apple, an orange, a handful of golden wheat, or any article of life, but the invisible in physical form? Stored up in fruit and grain and vegetables, yes, and stored up in coal and oil, is the power of the sun, the power to illuminate, and to give life, and to propel and to warm. We eat the food and the power of the sun is released in us for health and energy. I know it sounds absurd when we say that there was a time when a German transformed a dish of sauerkraut into a beautiful symphony, but he did, and what is more, the power of the sun in the kraut produced the energy and thought that were transformed into music. Hence

I have reasoned that this power from outside our world that becomes resident in all these physical forms of life, and has power to increase life in us, might be likened unto the energy of God which we call the Holy Ghost.

Of course, that illustration also dies, for we are dealing here with inanimate forces and not with persons, and the Trinity is composed of persons.

Then, too, I have played with the idea of the Father being pure mind, pure rational force. He is the Mind behind the universe. He is the Thinker in the ivory tower. He does not come down Himself. He stays in the tower but He sends forth those who share His ideas with the world.

Now a mind reveals itself in two ways: by speech and by action. On this basis I have thought of the Son as the Word, just as John did, and I have pictured the Holy Ghost as God in action, the energy of God seeking to motivate our world toward Godlikeness. Hence Jesus reveals what God is, what God thinks, what God wants, because He is the Word, the best expression of the Mind. Hence, too, the Holy Ghost is the energy of God, the influence of God, entering into persons and events, applying to life the thoughts of the Mind and the teachings of the Word.

There is more, but I have beat the bushes enough. Finite man cannot possibly portray the divine as it is, nor comprehend God's normal being. What is normal in the realm of divinity appears abnormal to humanity. The primary, beginning thoughts of God are so far ahead of our ability to absorb and understand, that it is not strange that we stumble where angels walk with ease and question where little angels nod their heads in complete comprehension.

Think as we may the problem remains, but thinking does increase our powers of reach and grasp. Seeking answers to such questions may not bring us to the pearly gates of the Divine Presence but it will create new highways and gateways in us, and give us a glimpse of the distant towers.

Of this I am sure: God's Spirit is not our private possession. I believe that God has spoken unto all peoples, that He has never left Himself without a witness. Wherever men have caught at the divine garment they have grasped and retained at least a few threads of rainbow beauty that stand as symbols of divinity. That was the conviction of both Peter and Paul. As Peter said to Cornelius, "Of a truth I perceive that God is no respecter of persons: but in every nation he that feareth him, and worketh righteousness, is accepted with him."[3] Hence, I argue that while we have more of the divine truth than any other religion, the religion itself, and the Christ who gave it, are proof enough that we do not have all the truth. God has spoken in China and India, Greece and the islands of the sea, as well as to Galileans and the citizens of Jerusalem and Rome.

By saying that, I am not saying what many seem to say, namely, that because there is some divine truth and beauty in other religions then all religions are equal and equally acceptable before God. Even a cursory study of comparative religions will demonstrate that Christ truly bears a name that is above every name, and that in our Bible we have truth in a measure not approached anywhere else. But I herewith reaffirm my belief that the Spirit of God has ministered unto all nations and races and that in all of them we find the footprints of God and the overtones of the Divine.

One of the controversial questions in this area is this: Is the Spirit of God in the Old Testament the same as the Holy Spirit in the New Testament? When John in the seventh chapter of his Gospel says that "For the Holy Ghost was not yet given; because that Jesus was not yet glorified,"[4] was he speaking of degrees or what? Was he saying what Calvin said, that the Holy Spirit had been operative from the beginning, but at Pentecost the Spirit was given in His full measure?

Without belaboring the point I feel we must affirm that God's Spirit has been in the world from the beginning, but was more active after Jesus was "glorified." That is why we say that we are now living in the Spirit-dominated period of divine history. The Father has planned, the Son has spoken, and now the Spirit applies and activates.

When we say that God is here or that Christ is near, we mean that we feel the divine Presence. But neither the Father nor the Son is here. It is the Holy Ghost that is here, and when we sense His presence, we feel the presence of both the Father and the Son.

In other words, if you stood in the presence of the Father or of the Son you would feel just as you do when you are with the Spirit. In the presence of Divinity you could not possibly know whether it was the Father or the Son or the Holy Ghost. Since they are the same in quality and quantity, your feelings would be the same.

But is there not an element of subordination in the Godhead? Many have asked this question, and I think a word should be said concerning it.

There does seem to be an element of subordination. The Son obeyed the Father. The Father sent the Son. The Son knew only what He learned from the Father. The Father possessed knowledge and powers which He did not grant unto the Son. The Son does not occupy the same position in eternity, He being on the "right hand." The Son now intercedes for us before the Father.

That which is true of the Son seems also to be true of the Holy Ghost. He, too, is sent. He, too, obeys. He knows only what the Son and the Father tell Him. It is His task to bring men to the Father. That last statement moves me to emphasize this point: The actual object of our worship and trust is the Father. Jesus came to show us the Father. The Holy Spirit now operates to bring us to the Father. Jesus said, "I am the way, the truth, and the life: no man cometh unto the Father, but by me."[5] Our destiny is the Father!

I believe in the Trinity, and I believe in the Holy Ghost. Let none confuse you by saying that the apostles created the idea of the Trinity. I believe the Trinity is resident in the Old Testament, even though no orthodox Jew taught it then or accepts it now. But the Spirit is active back there, and in a sense, so is the Son, for how else shall we understand the theophanies of the Old Testament, the strange appearances of "the angel of the Lord," "the angel of God"?

Jesus most certainly believed in the Trinity. No one has had more to say on the subject than He. And who can treat the subject as adequately?

Jesus most definitely believed in the personality and power of the Spirit. One of the chief purposes of His life was to prepare the disciples for co-operation with the Spirit. He wanted them to drink of the Spirit as the source of their strength, wisdom, and courage. Thus we read in the fourteenth chapter of John, "I will pray the Father, and he shall give you another Comforter, that he may abide with you for ever; even the Spirit of truth; whom the world cannot receive, because it seeth him not, neither knoweth him: but ye know him; for he dwelleth with you, and shall be in you. . . . These things have I spoken unto you, being yet present with you. But the Comforter, which is the Holy Ghost, whom the

Father will send in my name, he shall teach you all things, and bring all things to your remembrance, whatsoever I have said unto you."[6] In the sixteenth chapter we read, "It is expedient for you that I go away: for if I go not away, the Comforter will not come unto you; but if I depart, I will send him unto you. And when he is come, he will reprove the world of sin, and of righteousness, and of judgment: of sin, because they believe not on me; of righteousness, because I go to my Father, and ye see me no more; of judgment, because the prince of this world is judged. I have yet many things to say unto you, but ye cannot bear them now. Howbeit when he, the Spirit of truth, is come, he will guide you into all truth: for he shall not speak of himself; but whatsoever he shall hear, that shall he speak: and he will shew you things to come. He shall glorify me: for he shall receive of mine, and shall shew it unto you."[7]

Jesus began His ministry by saying to Nicodemus, "Ye must be born from above," or "Ye must be born again."[8] When Nicodemus asked "how," Jesus replied, "Except a man be born of water and of the Spirit, he cannot enter into the kingdom of God. That which is born of the flesh is flesh; and that which is born of the Spirit is spirit. . . . The wind bloweth where it listeth, and thou hearest the sound thereof, but canst not tell whence it cometh, and whither it goeth: so is every one that is born of the Spirit."[9]

During the evening visit to the upper room on that first Easter Sunday the record says that "He breathed on them, and saith unto them, Receive ye the Holy Ghost."[10]

But they did not receive the Holy Ghost at that time. Forty days later He said to them as they stood on the Mount of Olives, "John truly baptized with water; but ye shall be baptized with the Holy Ghost not many days hence. . . . ye shall receive power, after that the Holy Ghost is come upon you."[11]

And the Holy Ghost did come to them. Looking back to the startling events of that outpouring of divine power the disciples were not too sure just what did happen. Five things Peter remembered:[12]

1. There was a sound from heaven. It was not a great wind but it sounded like a mighty wind. Whatever it was, it startled them and made them heaven-conscious.

2. They were suddenly illuminated. Their hearts and their faces became radiant, so much so, that it seemed to Peter as if a flame of fire floated just above each upturned countenance.

3. They were filled with ecstasy. It seemed to Peter as if God had suddenly entered the room and had spoken and touched them. It was like old times when they were with Jesus. Their fears and forebodings dropped away like leaves in an autumn wind. They were excited. They shouted and praised God. They called down His blessings upon nation after nation, and race after race. They talked and slapped each other on the back.

4. They were new men with a mission. The world task to which Christ had commissioned them became concrete. The truths concerning Him and His mission to the earth were like wine in their bodies, moving them to talk and shout. They were eager to get started on the Kingdom road.

5. They ceased sitting and began standing and striding.

What happened at Pentecost? We will never know the full story, but we do know this: Peter was changed. One moment he was a silent man lost in prayer, and the next he was a mighty speaker for God. Being Spirit-filled he preached with sincerity and conviction and three thousand people were moved to accept the Christ as the Promised One of God.

Yes, Peter was changed, but not permanently. It was not long before we find him acting the coward in the presence of Gentiles and Jews. But having known the Spirit's power once, Peter could never be happy again save in the presence of Almighty God. Others were changed. Common men became uncommon men. Ordinary people became extraordinary people. Men were won to the new faith, and the Christian Church was born.

No wonder Paul said, "As many as are led by the Spirit of God, they are the sons of God. For ye have not received the spirit of bondage again to fear; but ye have received the Spirit of adoption, whereby we cry, Abba, Father. The Spirit itself beareth witness with our spirit, that we are the children of God: and if children, then heirs; heirs of God, and joint-heirs with Christ; if so be that we suffer with him, that we may be also glorified together."[13]

Paul had ample opportunity to see what the Spirit of God can do with a man's life. Nay, Paul knew from experience! He expected something to happen in the life of the man who became a Christian and church member. That is why he wrote the thirteenth chapter of I Corinthians. That is why he said that "the fruit of the Spirit is love, joy, peace, long-suffering, gentleness, goodness, faith, meekness, temperance."[14] The work of the Spirit was not merely to bring men to God but to build God into men, and Christians were not merely adherents to a creed, they were persons who wrote their personal religious history in terms of good conduct.

This, then, is the special work of the Spirit of God: To help us understand the teachings of the Christ, to help us attain and confirm those principles of body, mind, and soul that exalt righteousness and build for godliness, to challenge us in our hours of inertia and comfort us in our days of sorrow, and to daily give us power to live with kindliness of heart, clearness of head, and cleanliness of conduct.

The story of Christian history is the story of individuals made new in Christ through whom other lives are touched for God. It is Jacob the cobbler in Germany finding the reality of the Father in the Son through the Spirit. It is this same Jacob talking with Zinzendorf who restored the Moravian Church. It was through the Moravians that John Wesley, clergyman of the Church of England, was blasted from his religious sterility. During a storm on the Atlantic, he was filled with fear and was afraid of death, while the Moravians on board sang hymns of faith and praise. Through their faith and genuine zeal Wesley was later converted, and through Wesley God brought a great revival of religion to the world.

That is the way the Spirit works. He touches your life. Through you He seeks to touch other lives. Thus, the Church expands and grows, and thus the Kingdom comes.

Every Christian doctor should court the Spirit's blessing to the end that he may do his best work. So should the preacher, the teacher, the professional man, the businessman. Young and old should ask for His presence that they may grow into His likeness and into His revealing.

There is not a Christian in the world who cannot be a better Christian, a happier Christian, a more usable Christian, by surrendering himself to the guidance of God's Spirit. God is eager to bless you, and through you to bless others, but you must open your life to Him. Too often we resist the Spirit, we grieve the Spirit, we quench the Spirit. The result is spiritual inertia. Why not try living by the Spirit?

Is not this the proper time to pray:

> "Spirit of God, descend upon my heart;
>   Wean it from earth; through all its pulses move;
>   Stoop to my weakness, mighty as Thou art,
>   And make me love Thee as I ought to love.

> "I ask no dream, no prophet ecstasies,
>   No sudden rending of the veil of clay,
>   No angel visitant, no opening skies;
>   But take the dimness of my soul away.

> .   .   .   .

> "Teach me to love Thee as Thine angels love,
>   One holy passion filling all my frame;
>   The baptism of the heaven-descended Dove,
>   My heart an altar, and Thy love the flame."[15]

Amen.

CHAPTER ELEVEN

"I Believe in the Holy Catholic Church, But…"

(A COMMUNION MEDITATION)

ह**

BEHOLD THE TABLE of our Lord. How beautiful it is with its white cloth, the silver candelabra, the silver plates filled with prepared wafers, and the silver chalices filled with sacramental wine. Above the table and on either side, behold the white flowers that speak of the hills He loved, and in the center the white cross, symbol of His sacrament of love. One cannot look upon this table, so lovely to the eye, so significant to the heart, without sensing that here the sublime draws near to bless the ordinary, here God meets men with grace that forgives, and affection that lifts.

When we come to the Lord's Table on World-Wide Communion Sunday, we are reminded that we join with Roman Catholics, Greek Catholics, and most Protestant groups in observing the highest sacrament of Christendom, and we are one at His Supper. What better evidence of spiritual unity can there be than the centrality of this feast in all Christian brotherhoods?

Because we meet before His Table, I would have you pause and consider with me the meaning of this world-wide fellowship that actually includes all branches of the Christian family, "the holy catholic Church."

Where do we find these words? They are part of the Apostles' Creed. Did the apostles write the creed? No, they did not. There was no creed in the first century. During the second century creeds began their growth. It was essential that the Church have creeds for two reasons: to combat the unbelievers, and to convince converts. The creed we recite doubtless was born in the second century but did not reach its present form before the fifth, and it is very probable that it was given orally to new church members very much as we now initiate members into secret societies. In many ways the early Church was just that!

As a creed it is not all-inclusive. If we were writing a creed today we would add to this one some of the sociological elements of our Christian faith. The creed as it now stands is theological first and last; it says nothing of the joy and ecstasy of the early Christians, their fellowship, their evangelical zeal, their daring outreach, their happy, constructive home life. Apparently, the world was convinced of the superiority of Christian conduct at the time the creed was formed, even though critics were not convinced of the intellectual soundness of the creed. The Apostles' Creed is a theological statement and is incomplete on its sociological side.

In this great historic statement of belief we find the words, "I believe in . . . the holy catholic church." What do these words mean?

The word "holy" is a high word, a noble word, a word that wears a heavenly halo in its hair, a word that is redolent with religious significance, a word that bids us to remove our shoes for the ground whereon we stand is holy ground.

The word has several meanings. It means that which is entire, whole, complete, perfectly knit together. It also means that which is pure and without blemish, and that which is ordained of God and used in man's worship of God.

That is what the word "holy" means. But dare we say that our own church, or any church, is such a church? Who knows of a church or a denomination that is whole, complete, perfectly knit together, pure, born of God and used only for man's worship of God? I don't know of any such. It is as John Calvin has said: "In this church are included many hypocrites, who have nothing of Christ but the name and appearance; many ambitious, avaricious, envious, slanderous, and dissolute in their lives."[1] Then how can we talk about the "holy church"? We can, and we should, for while the existing Church is both wheat and tares, the good wheat is present; while there are both sheep and goats present, the Shepherd knows the sheep; while there are fruitful branches and fruitless twigs, the Gardener knows them all; while the net holds many fish, some good and some bad, the Master Fisherman knows which to keep. In other words, the holy Church is within the earthly Church, it is composed of those who are truly consecrated to Christ and are eternal in their loyalty to Him. This group within the membership of the Church is the holy Church, and whatever it lacks now it will gain in the world to come, and it is through this consecrated core of Christianity that God works for the saving of the world.

What then does "catholic" mean? Can we resolve it as easily? Can we separate it from its causes, and emphasize its proper uses?

The word "catholic" means universal, that which is everywhere, that which is ubiquitous. The early Christians used the word to emphasize the fact that Christians of all nations and races who professed Christ as Lord were members of the true Church; that the Church is one in Christ. Thus, the Church is catholic as sin is catholic, as salvation is catholic, as beauty and stars are catholic. It is thus that Paul thought of the Church. In the opening verse of his first letter to the Corinthians he says, "Unto the church of God which is at Corinth, to them that are sanctified in Christ Jesus, called to be saints, *with all that in every place* call upon the name of Jesus Christ our Lord."[2] To the Ephesians he said, "There is one body, and one Spirit, even as ye are called in one hope of your calling; one Lord, one faith, one baptism, one God and Father of all, who is above all, and through all, and in you all."[3]

Jesus expressed the same thought in His picture of the vine and the many branches, and John echoed it in his words concerning the great multitude which no man could number of all nations and tongues.

Not only does the word "catholic" mean universal, but it is now associated with certain Christian bodies, so that we speak of the Roman Catholic Church, the Greek Catholic Church, the Old Catholic Church, and the Anglo-Catholic party in the Episcopal Church. In this sense, catholic means that certain churches are united universally into a single organization which follows a particular prescription of liturgy and theology. Thus the word "catholic" carries the idea of uniformity. The Roman Catholic Church attains this uniformity through external forms; *e.g.,* all Roman Catholics must have certain things in common, and all must own the sovereignty of the pope. The Greek Orthodox Church gains its unity through mystical oneness in terms of traditions, and so forth.

In a very real sense all Christians are Catholic Christians, and a person can be a Catholic Christian without being either Greek Catholic or Roman Catholic. Why should we not refer to ourselves as Presbyterian Catholics, thus recognizing our relationship with Christians all over the world who follow our Presbyterian form of government and doctrine? And why should there not be Methodist Catholics, Baptist Catholics, aye, and Protestant Catholics?

We have not, and we do not, attach the name Catholic to our name, not because we are not catholic in our profession of faith in Christ, in our faith in the Holy Scriptures, in our world outreach, and in our hopes for the eternal Kingdom, but because we feel that there is no need of our using the word. All Protestants gladly and proudly and sincerely say the ancient words, "I believe in the holy catholic church," and joyously affirm our brotherhood with all members of Christ's family regardless of titles. To be sure we do not have a pope, nor do we agree in our forms, but we do agree in our faith in the Trinity, in the Sacraments, in Christ's power to save us from sin, and in heaven's gates; in the finality of the Scriptures concerning theology and conduct, and in the power of the Holy Spirit to guide, strengthen, and use us. Hence, the word "catholic" merely emphasizes our membership in the universal and eternal family of Christ.

What then is the Church? To some Christians the church is a building, a certain type of architecture. In reality the church building is a building built by and for a church, which means a congregation of Christians. The people are the church, and it is they who erect the building. The destruction of the church building does not destroy the church, for the church can erect another building for its use.

When we say we believe in the holy catholic Church we are not talking about buildings at all, but about people who believe in Jesus Christ as Lord and Redeemer. The holy catholic Church is a tremendous organization, bigger than the Roman Catholic Church, bigger than the Greek Orthodox, bigger than all Protestant bodies combined. The holy catholic Church includes them all. There are to be no denominational lines in heaven, and I doubt that God recognizes the lines we draw on earth.

When I stand before the Lord's Table on World-Wide Communion Sunday I am thinking of the Church Visible, the Church which includes all churches, a redeemed humanity in conscious union with God in Christ.

When I come to this Table I think of the Church Invisible, the Church composed of all believers who have completed life and are now with Christ in peaceful Paradise. My dead loved ones are alive. They have not ceased to be members of Christ's Church. They are more truly members today than they were when they lived on earth, and they know now, as they never knew on earth, what it means to be a member of God's eternal family.

When I come to the Lord's Table I like to think that Christ shall meet me here. I like to think that here He will bless me, take away my sins, and strengthen me for holy living. His holy body in me must in a very real way make me holy when I come to Him for forgiveness and for power.

When I come to the Lord's Table I like to think that my departed loved ones meet me here, for this Table is in a very special way the symbol of love that is deathless, of love that refuses to be victim to the grave, of love that makes us all, the living and the dead, one family forever in Christ.

When I come to the Lord's Table I am very conscious of the perfection of Christ and man's imperfections. Some of us are saved sinners and others are unsaved sinners, but all of us, Christian and pagan, are sinners before God, men and women, boys and girls, who stand in need of God's mercy, God's forgiveness, God's cleansing, God's guidance, God's power, and God's wisdom.

When I stand before this sacred Table I see my task as a minister more clearly than at any other time. It is not my task to stand where Christ would stand and condemn men to hell. It is not my task to shout and wave my fists at those who falter and fail. I need spend no time describing searing flames and bitter loneliness. My task is to open the gates of heaven so wide that the glory of God's home will flood the earth and thus convince man that there is a path of light and moral glory. My task is to tell men that while they may be sinners now they need not remain in their sins. I am not man's judge and jury, I am merely a man consecrated to God for the purpose of telling men that God has provided a way of escape for those who repent of their sins and seek His favor. Here in the church we offer to men that Bread, whereof if man eat, he shall never die.

Yes, I believe in "the holy catholic church." I believe she is the mother of us all, and I believe she is the door to heaven and the gateway to a better life on earth. With all her shortcomings and her shortsightedness, in spite of her imperfect leaders and members, God has used her, and is using her, for the saving of mankind.

The great Garrick was once talking with a famous Anglican bishop. The bishop praised Garrick for his great acting and asked him to explain the difference between the attractiveness of the stage and the pulpit. This is what Garrick said, "It is because I take fiction and make it sound like truth, whereas you take truth and make it sound like fiction."

Too often we make God's truth sound like fiction, but when we meet before His Table, and remember the facts of Christ's life and love, we are moved to resolve that henceforth, God helping us, we will believe, and will strive to make men understand, that God has spoken.

Let me say to all of you that God loves you. He gave His Son to prove it, and the Son died on a cross to reaffirm the fact. He rose from the grave for your faith, and lives today to give you power for righteous living. That is why we meet on World-Wide Communion Sunday in the presence of His Table. This is the highest evidence of our faith, this table of sacrifice, this table of redeeming affection, this world-wide fellowship.

Because we believe in "the holy catholic church," I have no desire, and the Church has no desire, to exclude anyone from the Lord's Supper. Regardless of your denominational background and affiliation, if you want to live a nobler life, and want Christ's peace in your heart, and are willing to look up and say, "Lord, Thou knowest that I love Thee," you are invited and urged to come to the Lord's Table and to partake with us, thus giving new meaning to the words, "I believe in the holy catholic church."

CHAPTER TWELVE

"I Believe in the Forgiveness of Sins, But..."

(JOHN 1:29-34)

ટે**

A MODERN THINKER, looking out upon our now not-so-progressive world of atomic power and atomic fears, says, "The greatest discovery of our age is . . . the rediscovery that Jesus *is* enough, that His redemption *is* adequate to all our mortal needs and our immortal longings; equal alike for personal security and social sanctity."[1]

It is strange, is it not, that the first Palm Sunday crowd did not sense the adequacy of Jesus! There were doubtless a few who understood, seeing with clearer minds and hearts the majestic deity in Him, but they were not many. Most of them shouted, "Hosanna; Blessed is he that cometh in the name of the Lord: Blessed be the kingdom of our father David . . . Hosanna in the highest."[2] Others asked, "Who is this?" The answer came back, "This is Jesus the prophet of Nazareth."[3]

"The prophet of Nazareth?" Three years before, John the Baptist, seeing Jesus coming toward him, had said to his followers, "Behold the Lamb of God, which taketh away the sin of the world."[4] For three long years Jesus had lived in the life of that little nation like springtime, and yet, the best that many could say about Him was that He was "the prophet from

Nazareth." Jesus might well have said to them what He later said to Philip, "Have I been so long time with you, and yet hast thou not known me?"[5]

He came to be the world's Christ, but they saw only a national leader. He wanted them, and all He received were some branches stripped from public trees. He wanted their hearts, but all that they laid down were their shoddy garments. He wanted them to give that for which God has always hungered — the love of man for God. God's hunger for companionship seems to have been the motivating force in man's creation. It was most certainly the sole force in man's redemption. God seems to hunger for our love even as we thirst for His.

This hunger of God is the strangest of all things to me. For its satisfaction He created the heavens and the earth and brought forth life and man. For it He has waited and worked for millions of years. For it He sent His only begotten Son, and the Son gave His life. God wants our friendship, our understanding, appreciation, affection, loyalty, and love. That is the story behind redemption. That is what we mean when we say that God has released us from the shackles of sin. He loves us. He even died for us. He set us free as slaves that we might be secure as His children.

Why things should be that way with God I do not know. Why should God be interested in people such as we? Few of us are good company for humans, let alone companions of the Divine! How this may be we can only surmise, but this we know: His love is real and royal in Jesus Christ. In Him God keeps saying over and over, "He is adequate."

Henry Scrougall of Scotland, writing in the nineteenth century, defined religion as "The life of God in the soul of man." That is the kind of religion we need. That is the kind we know our world needs. Without that kind of religion, and it most certainly was the religion of Jesus, there is no hope for the world. But how can we get God into our lives, how can God live in the souls of men, when the souls of men are little better than garbage pails? Though I hasten to say that they are often attractive, well-kept garbage pails. Must not something wonderful take place in man's soul before God can enter? Must not the garbage pail become, let us say, a flower pot? Must not the divine hands touch us and bid sin depart? Must not we see ourselves as God sees us, both with our sins and without them? Is not the vanquishing of sin in man the major purpose of God?

I believe in the forgiveness of sin because I believe in God. Why do I believe? I believe because I find Him real where daffodils lift their golden chalices along the edge of Winter's grave. I find Him in the blossoming of peach and pear. His presence is assured when dawn mixes her silver and crimson on the mighty canvas of the eastern sky or when the banners of sunset are so many and so rich in color that one is moved to stand in devotional silence. The mountains are like fingers pointing me to Him. The sea whispers that it is but His finger bowl. The laws of nature, chemical, physical, and moral, as we know them in the arithmetic of the heavens and the earth, and see expressed in poetic form in the wisdom of plants and birds, manifest a Mind behind all things with which we all must deal. Everywhere in nature I find signs that read, "He has been here." The signs of Him are too real to be dismissed, and while Science as such is not particularly interested in First Causes and Final Ends, we are, for something within us, something within the whole race of men, keeps saying over and over, "It is he that hath made us, and not we ourselves."[6]

In the beauty of the world I find God the Artist. In the laws of the universe I read the thoughts of the Engineer. In the moral laws of life I find the Person.

I cannot conceive of beauty being the child of chance. I cannot believe that there can be law without a lawmaker. I cannot believe that an orderly universe, the laws of which we discover and use but do not make, just happened. In the universe and world I find a Mind at work. Since mind does not exist outside of persons I argue that the Mind is a Person. I argue that after millions of years of careful planning God crowned His creative efforts by creating man. It makes no difference to me whether you believe man came by the Toonerville trolley of evolution or the jet plane called Immediate Creation. The fact is, he came. And what is this climax creature? He is a reed, but not just a reed. He is an animal, but not just an animal. He is a god, but not quite a god. When he tries to live on an animal level it corrupts his nature and he becomes less than man. When he tries to live like a god he finds that his wisdom is immature and his powers limited. When he tries to soar as angels rise he finds that his wings are singed and clipped. Man is at once the foulest and the finest creature of the world.

Above all else man is a person. He possesses traits and capacities not known to any other form of life. As a person he knows the Person behind the Mind that is evident in the universe. Since persons can only come from persons, man argues that God is a person, and that Person with person can meet. Man also knows that the Person is above all persons, not merely in time and position, but in quality. We are as it were synthetics, but He is real, and man instinctively feels that his peace and his happiness can only come from the Real. I presume that is why humanity in all centuries has

believed in God, worshiped God, sacrificed to God, and legis-
lated in God's name. The Person is the hope of all persons,
and while civilized and cultured man may educate himself
into self-worship and therefore into a neglect of the Person,
the vast majority of the human race raises its arms toward the
heavens and cries, "God be merciful to me a sinner,"[7] or in
the words of the more ancient worshipers, "Create in me a
clean heart, O God,"[8] "Wash me throughly from mine iniqui-
ty, and cleanse me from my sin."[9]

This reaching for the stars is more than a traditional gesture. It is man at his best. It represents the kinship between
man and his Maker. As Dr. Elton Trueblood has said, "The
beasts do not need a philosophy or a religion, but man does."[10]
Man knows that earth is not enough. There must be something else. God will not leave us in the dust nor will He permit us to be eternally soiled. Man has always felt that, and
feeling, has believed that wrongs may be pardoned and life
extended.

That is why the spirit-life has always fascinated man. It is
his central reality. He knows his body is of the earth earthy,
but the soul, the spirit-self within, may not it be cleansed and
geared for high ascent? May not the Person who created man
as companion recreate man for a new world?

Perhaps that is why Jesus taught that the soul-life is the
only true life. Soul-adultery, He said, is worse than physical
adultery. Soul-anger, worse than the striking hand. That is
why He taught that men ought to so use life that their bodies
would not corrupt their souls and eventually cast them into
hell.

When He died on the cross His final words were, "Father,
into thy hands I commend my spirit."[11] That is all that goes
on. We shall not take our bodies there nor the things of earth

that have made us important in the eyes of men. We shall appear before Him as we are as souls!

Because I believe that we are souls with bodies, souls that do not die when the body dies, I cannot believe that God, the Person, would permit us to enter eternity unaware of the dangers inherent in our sins. Since He made us to be His companions it is logical to assume that He would make provision for our cleansing and spiritualization before we leave this world for the world to be.

I believe He has. I believe Jesus is God. I believe that when I know Him, I know the Father. Not all of the Father, to be sure, for you cannot confine much of God in a human body and an earthly life. But I have seen in Him more of God than can be seen anywhere else in the world.

It is from Jesus that we learn the truths of redemption. The God who created man to be His companion has set a golden ladder in the earth whose top reaches into heaven. It was Jesus who demonstrated the love of God for sinful men, and it was He who made His cross the golden ladder to the sky. Thus all who desire to ascend must ascend by His cross, and in His company. That is why He said, "I am the way, the truth, and the life: no man cometh unto the Father, but by me."[12] The God who started us on the heavenward way has made adequate preparations for our cleansing through Jesus Christ. Even as He said to the prodigal, the street woman, the epileptic, and to others, so He says to all who trust in Him, "Thy sins be forgiven thee."

I believe in the forgiveness of sin because I believe sin is real. But what do we mean when we talk about sin? To the ancient Hebrew and the early Christians it meant choosing the wrong path, missing life's goal, slipping away from the truth, breaking divine law, failure to live up to one's best.

Who should know more about these matters than we who live in the twentieth century? Ponder the brutality of the last war. Think of the depravity of the concentration camps and Dachau. Talk to any of the service men who saw action and listen to what they have to say about the evil within our foes, yea, within ourselves. Or read Freud. See as he saw the cesspool of the unconscious life. Even the best of us harbor within ourselves a land of crawling thoughts and lizard-like desires. Marley, you remember, called this the "terrible impedimenta that rests upon the soul." Plato said that "there is at the bottom of the mind a sediment, a deposit of animal stupidity, which, when stirred up by the storm of passion, befogs the reason and blinds it. The wild horse in man runs away with his reason and the chariot of life is wrecked."[13] Dr. Leslie Weatherhead[14] says that we should think of being psychoanalyzed as we think of a serious abdominal operation, something to be avoided except in an extreme emergency. Why? Because of the horror that lies hidden within us all. We should not have to face it.

Modern man likes to scoff at what the older theologians called the state of sin, original sin, and the sinfulness of the natural man. But psychologists do not scoff. The stain is there and it is always a spreading stain. The unconscious is the ghost of the conscious, in fact, it is at times the soul's Dracula.

The little girl summed up mankind's conviction in these matters when she said, "Being good isn't any fun." But why isn't it? We know that goodness is constructive, safe, sane, sensible, and security-minded. We spend billions each year and employ countless millions to increase goodness in life. We say it is mankind's basic need. And yet, we do not seem happy being good.

There is in man a strange perversity that makes the not-so-good more attractive than the good. We spend our lives training ourselves to live below the best we know. Our lips pray, "Not my will, but thine, be done." Our lives say, "My will or else." God, looking down upon our struggle, wants us to have the best, but must leave us to our choices, saying to us as we are supposed to say to Him, "Thy will be done."

Sin is more than a hangover from evolution, more than the untamed animal in man. It is a state of nature, and every one of us has helped create and maintain that state. We know we are responsible.

Sins have been classified as:

1. Sins of Omission, the things we never bothered learning to do or, knowing, left undone.
2. Sins of Commission, the things we did which we should never have done.
3. Sins of Infirmity, the things we do because we are weak earthly creatures, not viciously, but habitually.
4. Sins of Secrecy, the thoughts and desires, the resentments and jealousies, the things we do inside that stain.
5. Sins of Presumptuousness, the self-sufficiency, selfishness, and self-will that make us ignore the divine will.

Sins! It is so easy for us to pick out the drunkard and the gambler, the rake and the robber. For two thousand years preachers have damned these poor fellows above all others, and yet the worst sins, the sins that anger God above all others, are the sins of so-called respectable people: false pride, self-sufficiency, snobbishness, social indifference to man's need, cruel prejudices, and all the cultured jungle ways whereby we crush and kill the spirits of men while leaving their bodies quite alive. Nothing in all the world is as bad as the self-righteousness of religious people. Jesus ate and drank with publicans and sinners, but the people He loathed, if I may use the phrase, were not these poor body-conscious people who were outcast by the "self-righteous" Pharisees themselves, those who felt that they needed no repentance.

Even a cursory study of the realm of sin makes clear the fact that there is none righteous. All have sinned and fall short of the glory of God — publican and Pharisee!

Washington Irving did not always think so. He was a faithful churchman even though he found churchgoing a tedious business. On a certain occasion he arrived at the church late, just as the confession of sin was being read. He heard it that day as if for the first time, and he was suddenly overwhelmed by the thought that he was a sinner in need of repentance just as other men. Falling down on his knees he prayed from his heart, and from that day to the day of his death, Washington Irving followed faithfully the Christ who forgives men their sins. I say to you, as someone has said to me, "Even at its best man's goodness is poisoned." Our good is never good enough, and we know it!

I believe in the forgiveness of sin because I know Christ does. Is He not the Saviour? Because I know Him I am neither foolishly optimistic nor darkly pessimistic. I refuse to be fooled by those who contend that man is really morally good and needs only a little tinkering to keep him going, and I will not follow those who say that humanity is totally depraved, that man is as bad as man can be.

I prefer to take the Christ attitude toward mankind and say with Isaiah,

"Wash you, make you clean; put away the evil of your doings from before mine eyes; cease to do evil; learn to do well; seek judgment, relieve the oppressed, judge the fatherless, plead for the widow. Come now, and let us reason together, saith the Lord: though your sins be as scarlet, they shall be as white as snow; though they be red like crimson, they shall be as wool."[15]

In the Apostles' Creed the phrase, "I believe in . . . the forgiveness of sins," comes after the phrase, "I believe in . . . the holy catholic church," and precedes the phrase, "I believe in . . . the resurrection." If there is no divine way to make men clean then there is no need of the Church. If sins cannot be forgiven then there can be no resurrection, since death is the blackest shadow of sin. Of what good is it for us to believe in God the Father Almighty, or in Jesus Christ His Son our Lord, if belief does not end in sins vanquished and life restored? If there is no forgiveness of sin, then Christianity is the greatest hoax ever perpetrated on credulous humanity.

But we need not mourn as those who have no hope. Forgiveness lies at the very core of the Church's life. As the Psalmist said long ago,

"If thou, Lord, shouldest mark iniquities, O Lord, who shall stand? But there is forgiveness with thee . . . I wait for the Lord, my soul doth wait, and in his word do I hope."[16]

I am sin-conscious as all men should be, but I am more salvation-conscious than I am sin-conscious. I know that our God is able to save unto the uttermost them that believe.

Two things are clear to me:

1. I would never have known what was wrong with my life if it had not been for the Bible. I knew I was restless, unhappy, lacking in purpose, but I did not know why. Only when I saw myself as a rebel against God, a man cut off from his best roots, a branch separated from the vine, did I discover myself. When I knew myself I knew that I was a sinner before my best self and before God.

2. If that had been all the Bible had told me it would have driven me insane or motivated me to take my life, feeling that life was hopeless. Thank God the Bible gave me more than sin-consciousness. It gave me Christ, and in Christ I found the answer to my fears.

Here is the Good News! "Thou shalt call his name JESUS: for he shall save his people from their sins."[17] "This is a faithful saying, and worthy of all acceptation, that Christ Jesus came into the world to save sinners."[18] "The Son of man came not to be ministered unto, but to minister, and to give his life a ransom for many."[19] "This cup is the new covenant in my blood" . . . "which is shed for many for the remission of sins."[20] "For God so loved the world, that he gave his only begotten Son, that whosoever believeth in him should not perish, but have everlasting life."[21] "There is therefore now no condemnation to them which are in Christ Jesus, who walk not after the flesh, but after the Spirit. For the law of the Spirit of life in Christ Jesus hath made me free from the law of sin and death."[22] "If any man be in Christ, he is a new creature: old things are passed away; behold, all things are become new."[23] "And you hath he quickened, who were dead in trespasses and sins; wherein in time past ye walked according to the course of this world . . . among whom also we all had our conversation in times past in the lusts of our flesh, fulfilling the desires of the flesh and of the mind; and were by nature the children of wrath, even as others. But God, who is rich in mercy, . . . hath quickened us together with Christ, (by grace ye are saved;) and hath raised us up together, and made us sit together in heavenly places in Christ Jesus: that in the ages to come he might shew the exceeding riches of his grace in his kindness toward us through Christ Jesus."[24] "My little children, these things write I unto you, that ye sin not. And if any man sin, we have an advocate with the Father, Jesus Christ the righteous: and he is the propitiation for our sins: and not for our's only, but also for the sins of the whole world."[25] "Herein is love, not that we loved God, but that he loved us, and sent his Son to be the propitiation for our sins."[26] "If we confess our sins, he is faithful and just to forgive us our sins, and to cleanse us from all unrighteousness."[27] "Whosoever shall confess that Jesus is the Son of God, God dwelleth in him, and he in God."[28] "Grace be unto you, and peace, from him which is, and which was, and which is to come; and from the seven Spirits which are before his throne; and from Jesus Christ, who is the faithful witness, and the first begotten of the dead, and the prince of the kings of the earth. Unto him that loved us, and washed us from our sins in his own blood, and hath made us kings and priests unto God and his Father; to him be glory and dominion for ever and ever. Amen."[29]

Hear it again: God is a person with a personal interest in us all; God is sovereign, not merely in physical power, but in mercy and love; God is love, and His love in us casteth out all fear: perfect justice must be perfect love; God is merciful: "There hath no temptation taken you but such as is common to man: but God is faithful, who will not suffer you to be tempted above that ye are able; but will with the temptation also make a way to escape, that ye may be able to bear it";[30] God is generous, giving us not merely better life here, but better and better life in the world to come; God is wise, knowing that we cannot cleanse ourselves, He has made for us a way to repentance, rededication, and redemption.

Oh, the wonder of the words, "Thy sins be forgiven thee"! The saddest word in the world is "Sin." The most beautiful word in the world is "Forgiveness." Christ's power to forgive is "the truth that makes all other truth true." It not merely asks that we believe something, but rather that we become something!

Joseph Fort Newton has observed that, "In our day a soft theology tries to disinfect sin by sprinkling it with rose-water sentiment, but to no avail."[31] Every student of the Bible, every person who knows the terror in man's soul, every person who knows Christ intimately, knows it cannot be done that way. It is not the disinfection of sin that we need, but its destruction, and only God in Christ can destroy it and make us clean.

Of all the benedictions of the Church the one shared with us by Jude stands as one of the best,

"Now unto him that is able to keep you from falling, and to present you faultless before the presence of his glory with exceeding joy, to the only wise God our Saviour, be glory and majesty, dominion and power, both now and ever. Amen."[32]

Let us read these words again,

> "Just as I am, without one plea
> But that Thy blood was shed for me,
> And that Thou bidd'st me come to Thee,
> O Lamb of God, I come, I come!

> "Just as I am, and waiting not
> To rid my soul of one dark blot,
> To Thee, whose blood can cleanse each spot,
> O Lamb of God, I come, I come!

> "Just as I am, Thou wilt receive,
> Wilt welcome, pardon, cleanse, relieve;
> Because Thy promise I believe,
> O Lamb of God, I come, I come!"[33]

O Christian brothers! O friends without Christ: "Behold the Lamb of God, which taketh away the sin of the world."[34]

CHAPTER THIRTEEN

"I Believe in the Resurrection, But . . ."

("DEATH HATH NO MORE DOMINION OVER HIM."
— ROMANS 6:9)

ࢭ

THE YEAR 1492 was a year of fear and pessimism. Many believed that the end of the world was drawing near and that it was only a matter of breaths to the day of final doom. The Nuremberg chroniclers left six pages in their manuscript on which to write the closing chapter of man's presence in the earth, so close did the death of the world seem to them. Men spoke of the brutality and chaos of life, the abominable wickedness, the times of lawlessness, injustice, war, pestilence, and famine to come. Times seemed so bad that many believed that the Seventh Angel was about to empty the seventh vial of its contents, thus giving birth to the horror of the ages.[1]

Such was the year 1492. Like our own day, it was a time of dark foreboding, a time of empty hopes and broken dreams, secularism and immorality. The golden tomorrows were dead, and nothing could happen save the total disintegration of mankind.

It was in such a time, in such a period of gloom and fear, that the good ship *Nina* sailed into the harbor of Palos on March 15, 1493, bringing a transforming message, a message that told of new continents, new adventures, new discoveries, new faith, new hope, new ambition. A new world had been discovered, and the old world found itself looking heavenward into the borealis lights of a new destiny. The old world was captivated and made new by the strangest of strange stories.

What happened as the result of the ship's arrival? The old was made young, the discouraged became the hopeful, the broken became the strong, and the skeptical cast aside his bag of tricks and took in place a compass and a sail. The day of lawlessness gave way to a day of good government. The Protestant Reformation came to cleanse the Church and revitalize and reorganize society. Faith in God became young and purposive, and instead of men looking forward with fear they began seeing the clear light of dawn on the far horizons. The possibilities of a larger, richer world got hold of men so firmly that they ceased to look back to glories faded, and instead they began to look forward to glories radiantly fresh and new. The maps were all changed, and so were the hearts and minds of men, and so was the world, and all because one came back from the untraveled seas, from the unseen shore, from the land beyond, with a message of promise and confidence.

It is thus Jesus returned from the dead. He is the little ship that sails into the harbors of today bringing the glad tidings of new lands beyond, and in His message there ought to be the sources of transforming faith for men and for nations. The pessimism and forebodings of doom should not imprison our day, or any day, now that we know that there are other lands, that there is a new world beyond the troubled seas of the life that is!

DO WE BELIEVE IT?

The "ship" has arrived. The "word" has been spoken. Do we believe it? Is the journey and the return meaningless to us? Has God's divine Christopher Columbus ventured and endured in vain?

Many a Christian, like Rabbi Joshua Loth Liebman in his book, *Peace of Mind,* ignores both the "ship" and the "message."[2] Dr. Liebman incorporated many good things in his book, but when he came to his chapter on death, the best he could do was to write a treatise on "Intimations of Our Immortality," for, not being a Christian minister, intimations were all he had. There was no resurrection in his Bible, no glorious Easter. There was no triumphant Jesus standing before an open sepulchre. To the Jew, the best of life is on this side of the grave, even as Solomon believed, and no ship and no Columbus have come back from over the vast gray sea with a message of discovery and hope.

I find myself in opposition to Dr. Liebman's statement, "All men today need the healthy-mindedness of Judaism, the natural piety with which the Jew declares, 'One world at a time is enough.' "[3]

That is what we now have, and with what horrible results. Most of our moral and spiritual problems rise from our lack of a Christian philosophy of death and immortality. We live as if this were the only world, and as if we had no power to win eternal life, or to determine the soul's destiny in eternity. We wash our bodies and put on clean and attractive raiment for the parties of earth; why do we do so little about getting our souls ready for God's party? Why do we spend our years welding our lives one to the other in human love when we could weld them together for all eternity in Christ? Why do we live as if this were the only real and permanent world, when as a matter of fact, it is the only false and temporal one? Our temporal-mindedness makes us materialistic, hedonistic, pleasure-mad, and lacking in incentives for noble Christian living. The Jew does not hold the secret of life's best. Such is not to be found in the Old Testament nor in the

Temple. It lives in the New Testament and is made real in Christ. What men need is not "the healthy-mindedness of Judaism," but rather the eternity-mindedness of Jesus and the early Church.

Dr. Robert E. Speer calls to our attention the occasion when an elderly wise man of Florence met on the street a youth of his acquaintance who appeared radiantly happy. When the young man was asked about the occasion of his obvious gladness, he said that he had just finished the university and was even then on his way to take his place in the leading law firm of the city. "Very good," said the old man, "and what then?" The youth replied that he intended to win fame and wealth and to achieve a great name in Florence. "I hope so," said the old man, "and what then?" The young man said he supposed it would be with him as with all men — life at last came to its end. "Yes, indeed," said the old man, "and what next?" . . . There was no answer.[4]

But there must be an answer. A man's philosophy of life is only as good as his philosophy of death, yea, it is no better. We Christians have the answer because we have seen the ship in the harbor and heard the good news. But do we believe it? Do we live as if we believed it?

I BELIEVE IT!

I believe it. The New Testament is convincing. The transformation of the disciples from men filled with fear to men filled with faith is convincing. The establishment and growth of the Christian Church is convincing. I believe it.

I am like a man on a journey, a journey that carries me through this life into life beyond life. My destiny is God. On the other side of death are heaven and hell, and heaven and hell are part of the life I now know. I have known both, and I know that I do not want hell increased. I have known heaven, and I want the moments and years I have known when heaven's glory shed its rainbow rays about my life, consolidated into an eternity of peace and love and service.

I have learned that one path leads toward God, and another leads away from God. If I walk toward God in this life, shall I not one day stand in His presence in the life beyond? If I walk away from God here, shall I not miss Him in eternity? Think you that men can take wrong roads to right destinations? Think you that we can flout the divine will and still escape divine judgment?

One day I must stand in His presence and give an account of the deeds done in the body. He will want to know why I ignored His Son, the Son's love and the Son's teachings, and the Son's offer of eternal life with Him. Even as Jesus Christ has divided all history, so shall Jesus Christ divide eternity. Here and hereafter we must do business with God.

The greatest event ahead of me is my meeting with God. He says that I am made in His image. What am I doing to that image? He says that He has given me all that is necessary for the cure of sin and the creation of righteousness. What have I done about the salvation He has offered? He says He has sent His only begotten Son into the world to save me from both sin and death. What have I done about the Son? He says I am an eternal spirit and not a temporal man. Am I ready for eternity?

On my journey I am conscious of high vistas of rare grandeur and low places of marsh-decay. I have known the joy of smooth driving over well-paved roads as they sweep by sea and city, mountain height and fruitful field, valley depth and city canyon. Often the journey of life has been as lovely as a June morning on the Blue Ridge skyway from which one beholds a world filled with the glory of laurel and rhododendron. But I have also known engine trouble, battery trouble, fuel line trouble, punctures and blow-outs. I have known old rough pavement, high-crowned slippery detours, and the treacherous stretches of red clay. The way has not always been June in the Blue Ridge, but neither has it been all detours and mud. In spite of trouble, heartache and headache, inconvenience and concern, I have reached many a destination, and I shall reach the last one, the one that is more important than them all, the one with God. It is this destiny beyond life here that seems to me to be of paramount importance. To attain my soul's goal, eternal fellowship with Him, life is worth its price in terms of highways and detours.

I have been born into this world in order that I may be born into that other and better world. Hence I must live for heaven beyond the earth. I must be heaven-bound, and not earth-bound.

God is not so much interested in my earth years as in my eternal years, not so much in society as in souls. Jesus came to save men from sin, but let us add that death is the victory of sin, and we are not spiritual victors until we have eternal life. Jesus came to save us for the eternal Kingdom, for life beyond death. The importance of this life, and His teachings concerning this life, lies in the fact that only by living here can we live there, and only by loving God here can we be ready for life there, and only by service to our fellow men here in the name of Christ can we condition ourselves for heaven.

That is the important feature in the love that makes us one in this world. There is in true love the potentials of immortality. They need only Christ and His love to become deathless. Here I am learning the lessons of heaven. Here I am being disciplined for immortality. Here I learn to live with God and serve Him that I may live and serve in the Kingdom everlasting.

Salvation therefore is not an earth program *except* in its beginning. We have come into being here in order to prepare for life there. Jesus came from heaven here in order to make clear the soul's destiny and the right paths thereto. If we follow the Jesus path, we cannot miss the Father's presence, the new heaven, or the earth made new.

The poorest and shortest part of Christianity is on this side of death. The best and longest period is beyond. We are here for a few years at best, but we have it within our power to spend eternity with God and our precious loved ones.

Life here, for me, is a matter of getting ready for my real life yonder. Part of my training here concerns getting ready for life's great occasions. The greatest occasion I will ever attend is the Marriage Supper of the Son of God, and shall I not be ready when the great day comes?

This learning, this getting ready, this dressing up, this living and serving, is a program for earth that can only have final meaning in heaven. Morality, spirituality, and noble character are vague and unsatisfying apart from God and God's promise of endless life.

My citizenship is in heaven. Some day I will die, and when I do I do not want to fall, but rise. Here I try my wings, but one day I shall really fly. Here I learn the fundamentals of life, but then I shall live. Here my love for God and for others is imperfect, but one day it shall be perfect; and if I receive such rich blessings from imperfect love on earth, what joy I shall know from perfect love in the world to be!

If all these things be false, if in this world only we have life, then we are of all men most miserable, and Christ's life here was a great mistake. If the benefits of God's love in

Christ are only these poor pseudo-spiritual years, if the beauty of love within my home and friendships is to become ashes after all, then God has no large and final purposes, and my soul is a tramp and not a pilgrim. But thanks be to God I do not have to so condition my faith. The grave has been conquered by Christ. God has promised me eternal life through His Son, and I shall not miss the path nor the destiny if I follow Him.

Every night when I go to bed, I thank God that each member of my family is secure, and that we are all under one roof, each in his own bed. When I waken in the darkness and cannot sleep, I invariably think of those who are part of my house and my heart, and we are one. It is a good feeling to rise in the morning and to sit down as a united family to the day's first meal. It is wonderful to be surrounded by loved ones.

Of course, it will not always be so. The years will take their toll, and separations must come, but oh, the wondrous truth that even in the separation of distance and death, we can still be one in God, looking forward confidently to the time when we will again be under one roof, and be one family forever. As the old gentleman said when asked about his love for his wife:

"The contract 'twixt Hannah, God and me,
  Was not for one or twenty years, but for eternity."[5]

ARE WE READY?

Hence we Christians should be majoring in living and minoring in dying. We should be learning how to live for all eternity, and not merely for our few years here. Some day the "shears of fate" must cut the silver cord that holds us and we must go when the bells toll, but when a Christian dies it is Commencement Day, not death, for he goes forth into life.

I have conducted many funerals in my ministry, but I have never buried a dead man, unless by that we mean one who has entered eternal life without faith in Christ. As far as the moment is concerned, all those whom I have buried are alive, the good and the bad. I have performed the last rites above their soulless bodies and have made a bit of earth sacred by tears and love and flowers, but I have never buried a dead man.

Earth is not enough for any Christian. We need immortality with God. We all want immortality with our loved ones. We want more than the hope of immortality in the minds of those who survive us here. We want more than immortality in terms of achievements. We want endless, improved life. We all want life with God and dear ones in terms of quantity and quality.

Earth is not enough. We talk and work as if all problems would be solved if we could make all men equal in income and living conditions. We seem to be mesmerized by the thought that a warless world would be Utopia. But suppose justice, mercy, and truth reigned in the earth this very moment, would it solve the problem of death and the tears of love? Even in a well-ordered society you would have the fact of death, you would still need Christ's teachings, and would still need His saving grace, for the major portion of life, the real life, the soul's destiny, would still lie beyond the gray seas.

I dislike the roadside signs that yell, "Prepare to meet your God," but I know in my more solemn moments that there must be such a meeting and that now is the only time I have in which to prepare. It is well for all of us to face the facts.

Dwight L. Moody once said: "Some morning you will read in the papers that D. L. Moody is dead. Don't believe a word of it. At that moment I shall be more alive than I am now. I was born of the flesh in 1837, and was born of the Spirit in 1856. That which is born of the flesh shall die. That which is born of the Spirit shall live forever."

That is the teaching of Jesus Christ. "Whosoever liveth and believeth in me shall never die."[6] Death not only had no dominion over Him, but it can have no dominion over us who are one with Him.

You and I are children of the Resurrection, "nurslings of immortality." Why, then, do we condition our faith in the Easter Christ? Why do we not live as if we were getting ready to live forever?

The one institution in the world that possesses the message of "the land beyond" is the Christian Church. Why do we not shout the message to the stars and to the ends of the earth? The ship has returned. The good news has been spoken with jubilation. The fault therefore is not with the voyager who came back nor with the good news He brought; it is with us who hear.

Right conduct is important. Moral values should be maintained. Social problems should be met and solved. The world ought to be made better than it is today. But these things are true only because we are people of eternal worth, God's people, new people, people who are getting ready for love that will never end and for life that shall never die. World improvement can only come through soul-improvement, and soul-improvement can only come through faith in Christ, and faith in Christ should prepare us for eternal life with God.

Say not, "I believe in the resurrection, but . . . !" but rather say, "I believe in the Resurrected Christ. I believe that my

Redeemer liveth. He is not dead. He is risen. Because He lives, I shall live also."

Let us pray: O Father God, Thou who didst bring back from the dead our Lord and Saviour, Jesus Christ; Thou who didst in the beginning bring life from the lifeless, and who in Christ hast promised eternal life unto all who are dead in trespasses and sins, take, we beseech Thee, the tears we shed and the love we share and mold therefrom a rainbow beautiful that it may hang above the names of those we love and mourn; and in the days when the deluge-waves of sorrow rise to engulf our little world, let us look up and see the bow of promise, and take heart and trust. We ask in Jesus' name. Amen.

CHAPTER FOURTEEN

"I Believe in
the Life Everlasting, But ..."

(JOHN 20:1-16)

ॐ

Do you BELIEVE in the life everlasting? Jesus did, and because He did, and because Easter affirms the fact of His own
resurrection, we meet to sing our songs of triumphant faith
and glowing hope. For the promise was not merely to those
who walked with Him then, but also to us who walk with
Him now. This is the glory of Easter morn: Christ is risen
from the dead and has become the first fruits of them that
sleep!

The dawn that ushers in this day of days lifts more than the
curtain of night. Behold, the sable curtain of death is itself
raised that we may behold the wonders of life that is inde-
structible in Christ. God was not only in Christ reconciling
the world unto Himself, but God was also in Christ *resurrect-
ing* the world unto Himself. God hates death. God loves life.
Hence Easter!

Easter's message is not the message of man. Chemists have
stated that when man is reduced to his chemical elements the
list would read as follows:

> Enough fat for seven bars of soap.
> Enough iron for a medium-size nail.
> Enough sugar to fill a shaker.

Enough lime to whitewash a chicken house.
Enough phosphorus to put heads on 2,200 matches.
Enough magnesium to make one dose of magnesia.
Enough potassium to explode a small cannon.
Enough sulphur to suggest that Lucifer is in all of us.

Ten years ago it was computed that man's chemical worth was about ninety-eight cents. Thanks to inflation we are now worth about $31.00!

But is that all there is to man? Is that all there was to Joshua and Jesus, Peter and John, Augustine and Francis, Calvin and Wesley, Shakespeare and Milton, Browning and Beethoven, Washington and Wilson? Is that all we can say about our loved parents who are now with God in Paradise? Is that all we can say of our loved ones who charm our hearts and make our homes places of radiant happiness? Is the saint of no more worth than the scoundrel, the patriot no more than the pirate? I say to you we are more than bodies, more than chemicals!

Whenever people come to me to have the pitchers of their hopes made full, I wish it were within my power to fill them with the crystal waters of Paradise. I wish I could make all men feel the reality of Christ's promises. I wish, oh, how I wish, I could make them hear His words as the woman at the well heard them, "Whoever drinks of the water that I shall give him will never thirst; the water that I shall give him will become in him a spring of water welling up to eternal life."[1]

How we need it! Life here on earth is too temporary, too transient. These wonderful bodies cannot withstand the forces of gravity and time. These amazing minds that link all life, and all things, dawn and rise like the day, only to end in twilight and midnight. We spend our years learning to love and to be loved, and yet our hearts are not immune to the ravages of time. Even when we are saints and saviors we know the agony of sickness and sorrow, adversity and age, dimmed eyes and blind death.

Surely this cannot be the full story of life! Surely there is more to it than this learning that all we have learned was not worth learning since it ends in silence! Why build up these ties of life if only death awaits us?

Deep within us all there is the groping hand that stretches forth to find another hand, and a voice that sings that it may be heard by a listening ear, and a heart that whispers to a heart that understands. We cannot accept the finality of the cemetery. It is contrary to every tie of life and every attainment of man. That is why we all hunger for Shangri-La, the place where we do not grow weary and old, sicken and die. The heart argues that there must be a place where springtime does not lose its rapture, nor October its autumn glory; where beauty is beauty still, and truth is truth, and love is love, and where the weaknesses of man never become great barriers between man and man, man and God!

Never is this hunger stronger than on Easter morning when the Rose Garden of the Resurrection is as real as earth and sky. Earth is not our home. We love its green sward and purple hills, its stately trees and radiant gardens, its fruitful fields, great forests, and mighty seas, its silver dawns and its crimson sunsets, its star-studded nights and its wind-kissed days, but it is not home. The Black Wrecker shatters our fondest dreams and breaks asunder the dearest ties. Here we are victims of the Hounds of Hell that track us through the years and finally bring us to bay like creatures of the night. In our happiest moments we find their footprints in the soft earth of daily experiences, and we are sad. But somewhere, and we all dream of it, there must be Shangri-La where the hounds do not howl in the darkness nor threaten the security of heart and home.

There are only four answers to the problem of death: annihilation, transmigration, immortality, and eternal life. Dark indeed must be the life of him who sees nothing beyond save the chill and silence of the grave. To believe in annihilation is to confess that there is nothing in us, nor between us, nor around us, that ought to live forever: no love, no beauty, no creativeness, no goodness. To me it is unthinkable! Nor do I find transmigration much better, for here we are born and reborn into the world, now a cow, now a crow, now a spider, and finally, a saint. And when I have lived victoriously through millions of existences my reward is — to live no more! To be absorbed into the universe itself as rivers are lost in the sea. Nor does immortality, mere survival and continued life, bring me much gladness. For if we are to live beyond in some dull, dimly lighted world, devoid of true companionship, and cut off from all that is human and divine, why live? If, as the ancient Greeks believed, a slave on earth is better off than a king in Hades, of what purpose and value is immortality? But it is so different when we come to the Christian teaching of everlasting life. The early Hebrews have nothing to say on life beyond death. Not even Moses, who knew the death rites and death hopes of Egypt! The prophets and psalmists speak of it more frequently and with clearer thoughts. But it is only when we come to Christian literature that we see the sun rising in all its glory to give new day unto mankind.

The best of those who preceded Jesus thought of death as a going down into death and a remaining there until the end of time. At the end of time they would be called forth and judged, punished or rewarded. That was the knowledge of Job, the opinion of Mary and Martha, the only wisdom of Peter, James, and John.

Jesus changed all that:

1. He taught that there is no break in living. Death does not destroy the continuity of life. We do not sleep in the earth. We do not sleep at all. There is for us no coma that dulls the mind and silences the life. "To day shalt thou be with me in paradise,"[2] He said to the thief on the cross. Elijah and Moses did not come from a dormitory! "Our God," said Jesus, "is not the God of the dead dead, but of the living and the living dead."[3] That is why He corrected Martha. He said to her, "Thy brother shall rise again."[4] Martha replied, "Oh, yes, I know that he shall rise again at the end of time when the resurrection takes place." Jesus replied, "I *am* the resurrection. You do not need to talk about the end of time. You must not think of your brother as sleeping in the earth or wandering around in a shadow land. I am the resurrection. He who lives and believes in me is already resurrected. He has already put off the bonds of sin and death. He is already living the kind of life we call eternal, everlasting. You may think that such a man dies like other men, but I say unto you that he does not die at all. There is no delay in his entering into joy and peace. There is more delay in a night's sleep than there is in what you call death."

2. Not only is life a continuity which death does not break, but the Christian life we now possess is the life that goes on living. Eternal life, everlasting life, is not something added to us after death. It is something we get here and take with us into the experience of death. Eternal life is not a mere extension of life, it is a quality of life. It is the God-quality of life. That is why John wrote saying, "This is the record, that God hath given to us eternal life, and this life is in his Son. He that hath the Son hath life."[5] Why? Because the Son is our only sure contact with the Father. If we want to know God

we must know the Son. If we hope to have the God-life, the everlasting life, we must get it from the Son. Only those who have the Son can have the life.

Jesus said the same thing, "I am the vine, ye are the branches."[6] Only as living branches on the living Vine can we grow at all, and only as we use wisely the life of the Vine can we be fruitful and escape the knife and the fire.

"I am the bread of life," He said. "I am the living bread which came down from heaven: if any man eat of this bread, he shall live for ever."[7]

Christianity has always taught this. We do not need to wait until death to find out whether we are going to gain heaven. Heaven is both a state of being and a place, but only those who develop the state of being *here* shall find the place there. If God's life is in the Son, and if this life is eternal life, then we can have it the moment we accept the Son.

Heaven for us begins when we become Christians. The Christian life should be the heaven life, and should be manifested in our conduct here on earth. When we die we leave only these bodies behind us. What we really have, what we really are, goes on without interruption into Paradise. Paradise as I conceive it is for Christians a place of heavenlike peace and joy. Immediately upon death we receive a body that will be essential for our needs in Paradise. It will not be the final and perfect body which shall be ours eventually, the true heavenly body, but it will be adequate for our needs. When time has run its course, when it is time for the new heaven and the new earth, God shall then call before Him all those who are of the heavenly heart and mind, and unto these He will give heavenly bodies for the new life. First we shall have Paradise bodies. Later we shall have heavenly ones.

As Jesus considered these things the following were clear to Him:

1. Death is both spiritual and physical. For the Christian, it is only physical, for the simple reason that he has received into himself God's Son, who thus communicates to the believer the heaven-life.

2. There is no sleep of death or sleep in death. Being free from the limitations of this present body we shall possess an alertness known on earth only at widely separated moments.

3. We shall not be disembodied spirits. We shall be clothed upon.

4. The final resurrection shall not be for us the raising of bodies from the earth, but the adjusting of the Paradise body for its heavenly existence.

5. Death for Christians is promotion. It is an ascendant way. It is a going upward.

If these thoughts be more than thoughts, if they be facts coming to us from the Greatest Fact of all human history, namely, Jesus Himself, then are we wise in living life as we live it? Here we are striving to be good doctors, good preachers, good businessmen, good farmers, good housewives and husbands, when we ought to be striving to be good men! Our vocations will remain behind us when we die, but what we are, whether we be doctors, preachers, businessmen, farmers, or what not, will continue, either as wings or weights. If this be so, then we must be good men, godly men, men filled with Christ and filled with the Christ-life. This will make us better in all our vocations, but beyond that, will prepare us, not for this world only, but for all the worlds that are yet to be. Here on earth we emphasize our vocations as if they were our religion, and we use our religion as if it were an avocation. This is not right! Our religion should be our vocation and our vocations should be our avocations, the divine in us should be continually rising to higher power, and the man in us should be changing to the divine.

Not long ago I asked a group of people this question: How big will you be when you die? Well, how big will you be? Here on earth we magnify our size by adding this thing and that thing to ourselves: bigger offices, bigger practices, bigger homes, better clubs, more social life. On and on we go, building ourselves up by using the things we must eventually leave behind. But when the things are taken away, when we are seen without the magnifying glass of materialism, when we are seen as we really are, how big will we be?

Jesus spent His life trying to help us see the importance of this question, and to see the fallacy of building bigger and bigger barns for bigger and bigger crops, while leaving the soul untended in its sparse pastures. He wanted us to grow and to be important within, in ourselves, without recourse to things and positions, and most of us have forgotten. Easter comes to put the question to us with new and greater force: How big are you — really? Physically, and perhaps mentally, you are big enough. Are you big enough in terms of Christian character?

A few years ago some of my good friends were on a hunting trip out in Wyoming. One night as they sat around the campfire, their thoughts turned to the more serious things in life, and it was then that the guide, a man of Will Rogers' humor and insight, said:

"When I'm through with this old clay house of mine,
When no more guide lights through the windows shine,
Just box it up and lay it away
With the other clay houses of yesterday.
And with it, my friends, do try if you can,
To bury the wrongs since first I began
To live in this house; bury deep and forget;
I want to be square and out of your debt.

"When I meet the Great Architect Supreme
Face to face, I want to be clean.
Of course I know it's too late to mend
A bad-builded house when you come to the end,
But to you who are building, just look over mine,
And make your alterations while there is time.
Just study this house — no tears should be shed,
It's like any clay house when the tenant has fled.

"I have lived in this house, many days all alone,
Just working and waiting my time to go home.
Don't misunderstand me — this old world divine,
With joys, birds, flowers, and glorious sunshine
Is a wonderful place and a wonderful plan,
And a wonderful gift to man,
Yet somehow we feel, when this cycle's complete,
There are dear ones across we are anxious to meet.

"We open the book and check up the past,
And no more forced balances — this is the last.
Each item is checked, each page must be clean:
It's the passport we carry our Builder Supreme.
So, when I'm through with this old house of clay
Just box it up — and lay it away —
For the Builder has promised when this house is spent
To have one all finished with the timber I sent

"While I lived here in this one — of course it will be
Exactly as I here have builded. You see,
It's the kind of material we each send across,
And if we build poorly of course it's our loss.
You ask what material is best to select,
T'was told you long since by the Great Architect,
A new Commandment I give unto you, That you love
    one another,
As I have loved you.
So the finest material to send up above,
Is the clean, straight-grained timber of Brotherly Love."

You cannot bury a Christian man. Nor can you resurrect
a body of clay. We do not leave our loved ones in cemeteries.
Nor do we look for the morn when the cemeteries will be
places of open graves. The resurrection of which we speak
is not physical for us. These bodies will not live again, whether we bury them in bronze or cotton. When they cease to
breathe, their usefulness is over. God has better bodies for
us all.

How shall it then be? It shall be like planting wheat in
the field. The wheat dies, but in its death it reaches an arm
heavenward, and in the hand of that up-reaching arm, there
is new wheat — like the wheat that died, to be sure, but new
wheat, and not the same as that which was!

My Paradise body and my heavenly body will, in some
respects, be like the one I now have, but it will be a body
lifted heavenward, a body ready for God.

"Beloved, now are we the sons of God, and it doth not yet
appear what we shall be: but we know that, when he shall
appear, we shall be like him; for we shall see him as he is."[8]

REFERENCES and ACKNOWLEDGMENTS

References
and Acknowledgments

ৰ্জ্ঞ

CHAPTER ONE

"I Believe in Faith, But ... "

1. Hebrews 11:3. (Interpretative translation by the author.)
2. *Man Does Not Stand Alone*, A. Cressy Morrison. Fleming H. Revell Company. (Other gases account for one per cent of the composition of air.)
3. Psalm 100:3. (Unless otherwise indicated, Scripture quotations are from the King James Version.)
4. Luke 23:41.
5. "When I Survey the Wondrous Cross," Isaac Watts.
6. Hebrews 11:4. From *THE BIBLE — A New Translation*, by James Moffatt. Harper & Brothers, publishers.
7. See Isaiah 1:18.
8. Adapted from "The Turning Point of My Career," by A. J. Cronin in *Getting the Most Out of Life*. Published by the Reader's Digest Association, Inc., Pleasantville, N. Y., 1946.

CHAPTER TWO

"I Believe in Prayer, But ... "

1. A. T. Welford in *Theology Today*, January, 1947.
2. Matthew 6:33.
3. Mark 8:36.

CHAPTER THREE

"I Believe in Love, But . . . "

1. Frederick W. Faber.
2. Luke 2:14.
3. I John 4:7-8.
4. John 11:36.
5. I John 4:8.
6. "Love Letters," by Mary Carolyn Davies in *Ted Malone's Scrapbook,* copyright 1941 by F. Alden Russell.
7. Matthew 5:48. (Revised Standard Version.)
8. *The Ten Commandments in a Changing World,* Isaac Klein. Bloch Publishing Company, New York.
9. I John 4:11.
10. Mark 12:30-31.
11. I John 3:17. (Slightly altered.)
12. I John 4:20.

CHAPTER FOUR

"I Believe in Loyalty, But . . . "

1. *Now to Live,* Ralph Sockman. Abingdon-Cokesbury Press.

CHAPTER FIVE

"I Believe in God, But . . . "

1. *Christian Doctrine,* J. S. Whale. The Macmillan Company.
2. This general idea is found in *The Case for Christianity,* by C. S. Lewis.
3. John 8:23.
4. John 14:9.
5. John 14:7.
6. *Christ and Man's Dilemma,* George A. Buttrick, p. 180. Abingdon-Cokesbury Press.
7. *Between Heaven and Earth,* Franz Werfel, p. 103. Copyright 1944 by The Philosophical Library, New York.
8. This idea found on page 119 of *Between Heaven and Earth.*

CHAPTER SIX

"I Believe in Christ, But . . ."

1. Matthew 22:42.
2. John 11:50.
3. John 1:29. (American Standard Version.)
4. John 1:14. (American Standard Version.)
5. John 1:41. (American Standard Version.)
6. John 1:45.
7. Matthew 16:16.
8. John 4:29.
9. John 7:46.
10. Mark 1:24.
11. Luke 23:4; Matthew 27:24.
12. Mark 15:39.
13. Colossians 1:15-17. (American Standard Version.)
14. John 3:2.
15. *The Character of Jesus*, Horace Bushnell, p. 36. Copyright 1866 and 1917 by Charles Scribner's Sons.
16. *Jesus and Our Human Problems*, Robert E. Speer, p. 13. Copyright, 1946, by Fleming H. Revell Company.
17. Mark 13:31.
18. Matthew 28:18-20.
19. John 10:30.
20. John 14:9.
21. John 9:4.
22. *History of the Christian Church*, Philip Schaff, Vol. II, p. 16. Charles Scribner's Sons, 1887, 1920.
23. *Ibid.*, Vol I, pp. 862-863.
24. *Jesus, Man of Genius*, J. Middleton Murry, pp. 7-8. Copyright, 1926. Harper & Brothers, publishers.
25. "Christ's Victorie and Triumph in Heaven and Earth," Giles Fletcher, Jr.
26. "In Christ the New Has Come," Max Warren, in *Theology Today*, January, 1947.
27. Galatians 2:20.

CHAPTER SEVEN

"I Believe in the Crucifixion, But . . ."

1. *Christian Doctrine*, J. S. Whale.
2. John 15:13.
3. Matthew 20:28.
4. *Things Most Surely Believed*, Clarence E. Macartney. Cokesbury Press.
5. Acts 2:22-23.
6. I Corinthians 2:2.
7. Romans 5:8.
8. Romans 6:23.
9. I Corinthians 1:17-18.
10. I Corinthians 1:23-24.
11. Galatians 2:20.
12. Philippians 2:5-8.
13. I Peter 1:18-19.
14. I Peter 2:24.
15. I John 1:7.
16. Revelation 5:11-12.
17. John 10:11, 15, 18.
18. I Corinthians 11:23-26.
19. John 3:14; John 12:32.
20. II Corinthians 5:19.
21. John 14:6.
22. John 11:25-26.
23. Acts 2:23.
24. Matthew 1:21.
25. John 1:29.
26. *The Case for Christianity*, C. S. Lewis, p. 43. The Macmillan Company.
27. "There Is a Green Hill Far Away," Mrs. Cecil F. Alexander.
28. "Our Christ," Harry Webb Farrington.
29. See I Corinthians 2:2; Galatians 2:20.

CHAPTER EIGHT

"I Believe in the Ascendant Christ, But . . ."

1. Acts 10:34-43.
2. The Apostles' Creed. Compare I Peter 3:22; 4:5.
3. I Corinthians 15:20, 54-55, 57.
4. Philippians 1:21.
5. Romans 8:35-39.
6. I Thessalonians 4:13-14.
7. I Corinthians 15:58.
8. John 20:25.
9. Acts 7:59.
10. See I Peter 3:19; Ephesians 4:9-10.
11. See *The Strong Name*, James S. Stewart; *The Gospel of the Hereafter*, J. Paterson-Smyth; *The Christian Faith*, O. A. Curtis.
12. *The Gospel of the Hereafter*, J. Paterson-Smyth, p. 58 ff. Copyright, 1910, by Fleming H. Revell Company.
13. I Peter 3:22.
14. *The Shorter Catechism*, Answer to Question 37.
15. Author unknown.
16. *The Gospel of the Hereafter*, J. Paterson-Smyth, p. 1 of Foreword. Revised edition, 1930, Fleming H. Revell Company.
17. I John 3:2.

CHAPTER NINE

"I Believe in the Judgment, But . . ."

1. *Things Most Surely Believed*, Clarence E. Macartney.
2. *The Christian Faith*, O. A. Curtis. Methodist Book Concern, New York.
3. "The Seekers," in *The Story of a Round-House and Other Poems*, by John Masefield. Copyright, 1912, 1940, by the Macmillan Company and used with their permission.

4. Hebrews 9:27.
5. Psalm 1:5.
6. Ecclesiastes 12:13-14.
7. Isaiah 11:3-4.
8. John 5:21-24, 26-29.
9. Romans 14:10.
10. II Corinthians 5:10.
11. II Timothy 4:7-8.
12. Matthew 25:31-46.
13. I Peter 4:18.
14. II Corinthians 5:8. (American Standard Version.)
15. John 14:2.
16. I Corinthians 15:54.
17. See Matthew 11:22-24; 12:36; John 5:22.
18. John 3:18.
19. Hebrews 2:3.
20. John 3:16.

CHAPTER TEN

"I Believe in the Holy Ghost, But . . . "

1. Acts 19:2.
2. John 10:30.
3. Acts 10:34-35.
4. John 7:39.
5. John 14:6.
6. John 14:16-17, 25-26.
7. John 16:7-14.
8. John 3:7. (See also A.S.V. margin.)
9. John 3:5-6, 8.
10. John 20:22.
11. Acts 1:5, 8.
12. Acts 2:1-4.
13. Romans 8:14-17.
14. Galatians 5:22-23.
15. "Spirit of God, Descend Upon My Heart," George Croly.

CHAPTER ELEVEN

"I Believe in the Holy Catholic Church, But ..."

1. *Institutes of the Christian Religion*, John Calvin.
2. I Corinthians 1:2.
3. Ephesians 4:4-6.

CHAPTER TWELVE

"I Believe in the Forgiveness of Sins, But ..."

1. *Where Are We in Religion?*, Joseph Fort Newton, p. 5. Copyright, 1945, by the Macmillan Company.
2. Mark 11:9-10.
3. Matthew 21:10-11.
4. John 1:29.
5. John 14:9.
6. Psalm 100:3.
7. Luke 18:13.
8. Psalm 51:10.
9. Psalm 51:2.
10. *The Predicament of Modern Man*, Elton Trueblood, p. 17. Copyright, 1944, by Harper & Brothers.
11. Luke 23:46.
12. John 14:6.
13. *Where Are We in Religion?*, Joseph Fort Newton, p. 19.
14. *Psychology and Life*, Leslie D. Weatherhead. Abingdon Press, 1935.
15. Isaiah 1:16-18.
16. Psalm 130:3-5.
17. Matthew 1:21.
18. I Timothy 1:15.
19. Matthew 20:28.
20. I Corinthians 11:25 (A.S.V.); Matthew 26:28.
21. John 3:16.
22. Romans 8:1-2.
23. II Corinthians 5:17.
24. Ephesians 2:1-7.

25. I John 2:1-2.
26. I John 4:10.
27. I John 1:9.
28. I John 4:15.
29. Revelation 1:4-6.
30. I Corinthians 10:13.
31. *Where Are We in Religion?*, Joseph Fort Newton, p. 18.
32. Jude 1:24-25.
33. Charlotte Elliott.
34. John 1:29.

CHAPTER THIRTEEN

"I Believe in the Resurrection, But . . . "

1. See *Admiral of the Ocean Sea*, Samuel Eliot Morison. Vol I, p. 4. Little, Brown & Company, 1942.
2. *Peace of Mind*, Joshua Loth Liebman, p. 134 ff. Copyright, 1946. Published by Simon and Schuster, Inc.
3. *Ibid.*, p. 143.
4. *Jesus and Our Human Problems*, Robert E. Speer, p. 165. (Adapted.) Copyright, 1946, by Fleming H. Revell Company.
5. "Hannah Jane," David Ross Locke.
6. John 11:26.

CHAPTER FOURTEEN

"I Believe in the Life Everlasting, But . . . "

1. John 4:14. (Revised Standard Version.)
2. Luke 23:43.
3. Matthew 22:32. (Interpretative translation by the author.)
4. See John 11:20-26. (Interpretative translation by the author.)
5. I John 5:11-12.
6. John 15:5.
7. John 6:35, 51.
8. I John 3:2.